The Bhagavad Gita
a verse translation

Geoffrey Parrinder

The Bhagavad Gita
a verse translation

 **SHELDON PRESS**
LONDON

First published in Great Britain in 1974
by Sheldon Press
Marylebone Road, London NW1 4DU

Printed in Great Britain by
The Camelot Press Ltd, London and Southampton

ISBN 0 85969 008 3 (cased)
ISBN 0 85969 018 0 (paper)

Contents

Geoffrey Parrinder is Professor of the Comparative Study of Religions in the University of London. After ordination he spent twenty years teaching in West Africa, and studying African religions in his spare time, before becoming the founder member of the Department of Religious Studies in the University College of Ibadan, Nigeria. He has travelled widely in Africa, India, Pakistan, Ceylon, Burma, Israel, Jordan, and Turkey and held lecturing appointments in Australia, India, America, and at Oxford. He is the author of many books on world religions and has a particular interest in Hinduism.

Preface

The Bhagavad Gita, the Lord's Song, is the most famous Hindu poem and scripture, and in modern times interest in its religious and philosophical teaching has spread to the West. Composed in verse, mostly a short metre of eight syllables to the line, in the Sanskrit language, the Gita is part of the Great Indian epic, the Maha-bharata, the longest poem in the world.

The Gita has been translated into many languages and there are several English versions, though few are accurate and some are almost unreadable. There is need for a new version, easy to read and faithful to the text, and the double aim of this new edition in verse is to provide a rendering that is as memorable and as literal as possible. In this way many passages from the Gita can be learnt, in simple English verse forms, while keeping close to the words and meaning of the original. The Gita is not always easy to understand; there are references to names and places, and difficult passages that need some explanation, and so marginal notes are provided for the general reader.

The Gita opens at Kuru-kshetra, the battlefield of Kuru, near modern Delhi. This is taken as a symbol of the Field of Right (*dharma*), and the story rapidly advances to discussion of action and inaction, of 'human being, eternity and God'. Two armies face each other, the Kauravas or Kurus and the Pandavas or sons and allies of Pandu. The King of the Kurus, blind Dhrita-rashtra, sits beside the battlefield and his charioteer, Samjaya, tells him of the actions and discussions that take place. The early verses contain names of heroes and their weapons that are of little importance for understanding the Gita. The reader may omit these and begin at verses 20 or 27, in chapter 1, where the story develops. The inner Gita, the Lord's Song, begins at 2, 11. The warrior Arjuna, third prince of the five Pandu brothers, is filled with doubts and compassion before the battle. Kurus and Pandus are cousins and it is wrong for them to kill each other, so Arjuna refuses to do his soldier's duty. Arjuna's charioteer is the god Krishna, who answers this and many other problems in his Song that follows.

The Bhagavad Gita

1

Arjuna's Despair

Dhrita-rashtra said:

1 Across the Field of Righteousness
on Kuru-field my faithful men
encountering the Pandavas
prepared to fight—what happened then?

Two armies meet and
the blind king asks for
news. Kuru-field
symbolizes the Field of
Right or Duty (*dharma*).
It is the battle of life.

Samjaya said:

2 Observing how the Pandu host
was organized Dur-yodhan' went
along to where the Teacher stood
and tho' a prince made this lament:

His charioteer tells how
the king's son addresses
Drona, Teacher of both
armies, and names some
of the opposing Pandu
leaders

3 Look at this tremendous army
of Pandu's people, Learned One,
distributed in row on row
by your wise pupil, Drupad's son.

4 Fighters like Bhima and Arjuna
expert in archery are here,
Yuyu-dhana and Virata
and Drupada a great charioteer.

Drupada, a king allied to
the Pandus. Bhima and
Arjuna, second and third
of the five sons of Pandu.
The other names are of
allied heroes

5 Dhrishta-ketu, Cheki-tana,
the king of Kashi, the masterful,
Purujit and Kunti-bhoja,
and the Shibi-king, like a human bull.

Kashi is Benares

6 There's heroic Yudha-manyu,
Draupadi's sons and Subhadrā's,
riding by virile Uttamaujas
and all of them in massive cars.

Now heroes on the Kuru
side. Drona was a
Brahmin priest, twice-
born by investiture

7 But of our own distinguished men,
   Best of the Twice-born, learn from me
   as the chiefs of my battalions
   I indicate distinctively.

8 You yourself, Bhishma and Karna,
   with Kripa victorious in war,
   while Ashva-tthaman and Vikarna
   and Sauma-datti ride before.

9 And many another warrior
   is getting ready to risk his life,
   as with various arms and weapons
   they exercise their skill in strife.

A play on the names of
opposing champions,
Bhishma was the more
experienced

10 Altho' our troops are not enough
    in number yet Bhishma stands as guard,
    while their contingents are enough
    and also Bhima stands as guard.

11 Therefore in all activities
    stationed in every company
    each one of you be resolute
    to guard our Bhishma specially.

Bhishma sounds the call
to battle. The conch-shell
is still blown in acts of
worship

12 So to encourage him again
    Bhishma, the senior Kuru-lord,
    powerfully blew his conch-shell
    and like a lion loudly roared.

13 Then the conches and the cymbals
    sounded together all around,
    drums and kettle-drums and trumpets
    producing a tumultuous sound.

The two chief figures of
the Gita appear. Krishna
is the divine charioteer of
prince Arjuna

14 Foremost in a mighty chariot
    harnessed to horses white as snow
    Lord Krishna stood with Arjuna
    and both made heavenly conches blow.

15 Arjuna blew the God-given shell
and Krishna sounded Demon-bone
while wolfish Bhima of fearful deeds
howled thro' the massive Lotus-tone.

16 King Yudhi-shthira, son of Kunti,
played on the shell of Endless Power,
Nakula blew on Dulcet-notes
and Saha-deva on Jewel-flower.

Yudhi-shthira was
claimant to the throne,
eldest son of Pandu,
brother of Arjuna and
these other heroes

17 That great archer the King of Kashi
with Shikhandin in a great vehicle,
Dhrishta-dyumna and Virata
with Satyaki the invincible,

18 Drupada and sons of Draupadi
gathered together there, O king,
with mighty-armed Subhadra's son
and one by one made their conches ring.

19 The hearts of Dhrita-rashtra's men
were smitten by the noise and then
above the earth and from the sky
the tumult echoed swelling high.

20 At this the ape-bannered Arjuna
when the arrows began to go
saw Dhrita-rashtra's sons arrayed
and firmly lifted high his bow.

Arjuna bore the crest of
a monkey on his chariot.
He requests Krishna to
give him a closer view of
the opposing forces

21 Turning towards the Blessed Lord
he quickly uttered words like these:
Unshaken One, direct my car
and halt between both companies,

22 Till I have scrutinized these men
assembled there and keen to fight
and note before the battle starts
the ones I should especially smite.

23 I would scan the people gathered there
   eager that conflict should be done,
   who wage such war and hope to please
   Dhrita-rashtra's evil-minded son.

24 Being addressed by Arjuna
   therefore Lord Krishna drove him far
   until between the rival ranks
   he halted their superior car.

25 In the face of Bhishma and of Drona
   and every assembled king
   he cried: See yonder Arjuna
   where these Kurus are gathering.

26 Teachers, grandfathers and fathers
   were stationed there and Arjun' saw
   with his uncles, sons and brothers,
   grandsons and comrades and many more

Both armies contained
many relatives of Arjuna
so that he despaired at the
prospect of fratricidal
battle

27 Fathers-in-law and also friends
   were found in both the companies,
   and Arjun' noting on either side
   that all were relatives of his,

28 Quickly became compassionate
   and in despondency he spoke:
   O Krishna, those who want this war
   I recognize as my own folk.

The hero's body is
weakened, not by fear
but by portents of the
destruction of social
order

29 My body trembles and my arms
   begin to fall and legs to bend,
   my mouth becoming dry and now
   my hair is standing up on end.

30 My skin is burning like a fire
   my mind astray beyond my will,
   my bow is slipping from my hand,
   I can't continue standing still.

31 Then I see that all the omens
   are showing evil lies before
   and I prophesy no happiness
   if I kill my relatives in war.

32 I am not seeking victory
   for selfish joy or sovereignty,
   what would I do with a kingdom?
   what use would life or pleasure be?

33 But those whose good we do desire,
   their joy and rightful royal sway,
   appear with us in battle line
   yet throwing life and wealth away.

34 And yonder teachers, sons and fathers,
   grandfathers and grandsons as well,
   with uncles and fathers-in-law
   and brothers-in-law I should repel.

35 Yet I do not wish to kill the foe
   even tho' I myself am slain,
   not for the rule of all three worlds
   and very much less for earthly gain.

The three worlds are
heaven, earth, and hell,
and none is worth
destruction of the Right

36 If we killed Dhrita-rashtra's men
   would any happiness be ours?
   surely evil would come on us
   if we destroyed these murderers.

37 Therefore we should not try to kill
   Dhrita-rashtra's soldiers, our very kin,
   for having killed our relatives
   what satisfaction could we win?

38 Even if their minds are blinded
   by greed thro' which they fail to see
   the crime in injury to friends
   and sin that destroys a family,

B

39 Yet we should know enough to shun
the wickedness that would be done,
since we can clearly see herein—
to destroy a family is sin.

War brings destruction of
eternal law or right
(*sanatana dharma*). The
men are killed, women
marry into other classes,
and social order is broken

40 When a family is ruined
eternal family laws collapse,
the family is overwhelmed
by lawlessness when customs lapse.

41 Whenever lawlessness prevailed
family women were then defiled,
and when the women were to blame
a mixture of the classes came.

Family disruption means
neglect of offerings to the
dead and they fall to a
lower state

42 Such mixture only leads to hell
for destroyers and the family,
since their fathers are degraded
when food and drink fail ritually.

43 This family-destroying sin
makes the mixture of class begin,
the laws of birth are being destroyed
and eternal family laws are void.

44 When laws of family are annulled
the men responsible will dwell,
at least as we have always heard,
and that is sure, in deepest hell.

Heard, or taught, from
the scriptures

45 Alas, that for a ruler's joys
we had resolved, inspired by greed,
to slaughter all our relatives,
a monstrous and an evil deed!

46 Yet if Dhrita-rashtra's men come armed
and kill me in hostility,
when I am passive and unarmed
that is the safer course for me.

47 Arjuna said this in the fight
   and sat down on the chariot seat,
   dropping his arrows and his bow
   because his heart was struck with woe.

The hero decides not to
fight, rather than destroy
right and society by war

SO ENDS
THE FIRST CHAPTER
AND ITS NAME IS
*the Yoga of
Arjuna's Despair*

2
Theory

Krishna reproaches Arjuna for cowardice, and he explains his problem further. Then Krishna expounds the theory of the eternal and indestructible soul

Samjaya said:

1 Compassion captured Arjuna,
and as his eyes with tears were blurred
to him in his despondency
the Blessed Krishna spoke this word:

The Blessed Lord said:

2 Whatever in this time of danger
has given you faintheartedness?
both ignoble and inglorious
which cannot win a heavenly place.

3 It is not proper for you to yield
to cowardly unmanliness.
Get up and banish from your heart
this foolish petty feebleness.

Arjuna said:

4 Can I go to war with Drona
or even Bhishma, Blessed Lord,
by shooting with my darts at those
who both are noble men adored?

The metre lengthens for four verses, to repeat objections in a higher tone. Is it right to kill teachers even if they are greedy?

5 Far better in this world share beggar's food
than kill my teachers even when their mood
is seeking wealth, for if they die thro' me
the food I eat would all be stained with blood.

6 I cannot understand the better way,
for them to slay us or for us to slay,
we would not want to live by slaughtering
yon Dhrita-rashtra's men in their array.

7 My troubled mind does not discern the Right,
   I come as your disciple for the light,
   my being weakened by this sympathy
   tell me the better course and definite.

8 Whatever remedy that could dispel
   the grief that dulls my sense I cannot tell,
   not even if I win unrivalled rule
   on earth and lordship of the gods as well.

Samjaya said:

9 This is what Arjuna replied,
   who always scorched the foe before,
   told Krishna: 'I will never fight',
   and then he spoke to him no more.

Foe-scorcher, a title of
Arjuna

10 And Krishna answered in these words
    with the semblance of a gentle smile
    as Arjuna despondently
    between the armies sat awhile.

The serene smile of the
all-knowing deity

The Blessed Lord said:

11 You grieve for those you should not mourn
    and yet some wise words you have said!
    But really wise men never mourn
    either the living or the dead.

Krishna begins his Song,
the Bhagavad-Gita. The
tone rises from details of
battle and people to
eternal problems

12 At no time did I not exist,
    nor you, nor any present kings,
    and we shall never cease to be
    in any future happenings.

Four reasons are given for
fighting, and for action in
general. The first is that
the soul is immortal.
Both God and men are
eternal and indestructible

13 The soul located in a body
    discovers childhood, youth and age,
    then coming to another body
    does not perplex the steady sage.

The soul passes on from
one body to another by
reincarnation

14 Contacts from material objects
   bring heat and cold, and joy and woe,
   you must learn to put up with them,
   impermanent they come and go.

15 The man who is unmoved by these
   sees pain and pleasure equally,
   that steadfast man is really wise
   and fit for immortality.

16 For what *is not* does not become
   and that which *is* can never cease,
   the boundary between the two
   is seen by one who truly sees.

The dividing-line between
existent and non-existent,
or the truth about both, is
seen by men of real vision

17 Yes, That is indestructible
   by which this universe was spun,
   that imperishable being
   is not destroyed by anyone.

'That', the universal Soul
or Self, spins or pervades
'this', the world

18 They say these bodies have an end
   for this eternal embodied soul,
   but That one cannot comprehend
   so fight, 'tis indestructible.

The soul cannot slay or be
slain, a famous verse from
the Katha Upanishad 2, 19

19 Both he who thinks that *this* can kill
   and he who thinks that *this* is killed,
   have neither truly understood,
   this does not kill, is never killed.

In higher tone and longer
metre, see Katha 2, 18.
The soul does not come
to be, it is

20 He never dies and never born is he,
   came not to being and never comes to be,
   primeval, in the body's death unslain,
   unborn, eternal, everlastingly.

21 Eternal and indestructible,
   this is unborn and unchangeable,
   and when a man knows this how may
   he kill, whom will he cause to slay?

22 A man his worn out garments laying by   Long metre
some different and newer clothes will try
and thus the embodied soul takes other forms
when it discards the worn out ones that die.

23 *This* is never cut by weapons   The untouchable state
and *this* by fire is never burned,   of the true self
this is never wet by water
and *this* is never dried by wind.

24 'Tis never cut and never burnt
not ever wet or ever dry,
eternal, ever-present, firm,
this primal one, immovably.

25 *This* is unmanifest, unchanged,
and *this* they say is not conceived,
and knowing it to be like that
for sake of it do not be grieved.

26 If you think it ever dying   The second reason for
or if as constantly reborn   fighting, and facing death,
yet even so for such a one   is that what dies will be
you never should have cause to mourn.   born again and so grief is
    mistaken

27 Birth is certain for one who dies
and death is sure for one that's born,
this thing is unavoidable
therefore you must not ever mourn.

28 Origins of things are unmanifest   The middle of life is
yet manifest their middle is,   visible but not its
the endings are unmanifest   beginning or end
but why should you lament at this?

29 Someone beholds him as a wonder rare,   Long metre. It is a rare
in wonder may another him declare,   privilege to see the soul,
as rarest wonder one more hears of him   or one who sees it is
yet having heard none knows him whatsoe'er.   marvellous, or sees it as
    marvellous. Katha 2, 7:
    wonderful is he who
    declares, wins and knows
    him

30 The embodied soul eternally
   abides unslain in everyone
   so because of any being
   no lamentation must be done.

The third reason for action
is that Arjuna's class duty
requires him to act as a
warrior

31 Look then to your proper Duty
   and you will have no cause for fright,
   soldiers have nothing better here
   than Duty that demands a fight.

32 Presented by a lucky chance
   appears a heavenly open door,
   fortunate are the warriors
   who get involved in such a war.

33 But if you neglect this conflict
   which Duty says you must fulfil
   abandoning your proper Duty
   and honour you will come to ill.

Fourthly, the soldier will
be accused of cowardice
if he runs away, and all
men must do their own
duty

34 Many people in every breath
   will tell of your undying shame,
   dishonour that is worse than death
   to a warrior of noble fame.

35 The mighty charioteers will think
   that cowardice kept you back from fight
   and those who highly honoured you
   in the past will come to hold you light.

36 Many words that should not be said
   your evil-wishers now will say
   maligning your capacity
   and what could be more grievous, pray?

37 If you die you go to heaven
   and if you win the earth's your lot,
   therefore get up and struggle on
   remaining firm and resolute.

38 Consider equal joy and pain,
   victory, defeat, and loss and gain,
   so now prepare yourself for war
   and yet receive no evil stain.

39 From Reason-theory comes this wisdom
   now Discipline of practice hear,
   integrated by such wisdom
   the bonds of action disappear.

The battle is left aside,
and from the Theory of
the indestructible soul the
argument moves to the
Method of Discipline.
This is Yoga, yoking,
practice of self-control,
integration of self

40 In this no enterprise can fail
   and no appearance of reverse,
   just a little of this Duty
   will liberate from dreadful loss.

41 In this world that mind is single
   whose nature is firmly resolute,
   but never-ending and many-branched
   are the minds of the irresolute.

42 Undiscerning people utter
   many a kind of flowery word,
   both relishing the scripture verse
   and saying nothing else is heard.

Before expounding the
Method of Discipline,
from verse 47, some
other ways are criticized

43 Lustful souls intent on heaven
   the various ritual acts maintain
   aiming at goals of joy and power
   and as result of works are born again.

Their soul or nature is
desire, their goal is
heaven, but they are
reborn

44 Those who cling to joy and power
   deluded in their speech of wit
   have minds not firmly resolute
   for concentration never fit.

45 Scripture deals with three Qualities,
   but from these Qualities break free,
   stay firm in the Good, free from the Pairs,
   self-ruled, without gain or surety.

The Veda scriptures
treated of three Qualities
or Strands of nature:
Goodness, Passion, and
Darkness, see 14, 5f.
Pairs or Dualities are
pleasure-pain, gain-loss,
etc. One should be
detached from all
Qualities and Pairs

46 Useful as a tank of water
when all around the water lies,
there's no more in all the Veda
for any Brahmin truly wise.

Do your duty, without
seeking rewards. Work,
and avoid inaction

47 Fix interest not on results
but on your work as done, no less,
make not your motive fruits of work
nor be attached to worklessness.

The Discipline taught here
is detached action, and
integration of self, in
which all gain is evenness
or indifferent

48 Perform your work well disciplined
unmoved by failure or success
by abandoning attachment,
for Discipline is an evenness.

49 Activity is inferior
to any integrated mind,
those who seek rewards are wretched
so refuge should be sought in mind.

Both good and bad actions
can bring attachment to
rewards, but disciplined
action brings freedom

50 A man of integrated mind
abandons deeds both good and ill,
control yourself in discipline
for discipline of work is skill.

51 Wise men of integrated mind,
who all rewards of acts resigned,
released from transmigration's chain
go to the place that is free from pain.

52 Past the jungle of delusion
your mind eventually transferred
you will then attain aversion

Heard, traditional teaching

to what was 'heard' or may be 'heard'.

Integration of self
through the discipline
of Yoga

53 When averse to 'heard' tradition
unmoving will your mind remain
motionless in concentration
to integration you attain.

Arjuna said:

54 What marks the man of steady thought
who stays in concentration caught?
how does the steady thinker talk,
how does he sit, how should he walk?

The closing verses of this
chapter describe the
actions and nature of the
man of stabilized wisdom

The Blessed Lord said:

55 He who abandons all desires
that preying in the mind may be,
himself content in the self alone
he has stabilized mentality.

Self, soul (*atman*), an
important and ambiguous
word, used reflexively of
oneself, of true self or
soul, and of universal
Self or Soul

56 With reason unperturbed in sorrow
when passion, fear and wrath are nought,
having lost desire for pleasures
he is called a sage of steady thought.

57 He who has desire for nothing,
is not pleased nor yet antagonized
by getting this good or that ill
his mentality is stabilized.

58 A man has firm mentality
when all the senses he withdraws
from their objects, as a tortoise
from round about pulls back its claws.

59 From the embodied one who fasts
the objects of the senses flee
in all but taste—yet taste goes too
if once the Highest he can see.

One may renounce food
but the flavour remains
(see 3, 6), yet all desire
vanishes in the vision of
the Highest

60 For even in a striving man
altho' a wise discerning man
the impetuous forces of the sense
bear reason off by violence.

Desire can overwhelm
reason, but the Lord is
the object and aid of
meditation, see 6, 14

61 Whoever is intent on me
with all his senses tranquillized,
sitting down and integrated,
his mentality is stabilized.

62 What will bring about attachment
is when one ponders sensual things,
desire arises from attachment
and from desire fierce anger springs.

63 From such anger comes delusion
and from delusion memory's lost,
loss of memory brings loss of mind,
one perishes when the mind is lost.

64 One self-controlled and separate,
by ruling self, from lust and hate,
whose senses act on objects, he
proceeds to find serenity.

The senses act on physical
objects but the higher self
is detached and serene

65 In serenity all troubles
are brought to nothing he will find,
speedily the tranquil thinker
achieves stability of mind.

66 There is no right mind without discipline,
the undisciplined has no power within,
without such power he has no peace,
and with no peace can he find bliss?

67 The senses quickly go astray
and scatter one's mentality
whenever thoughts go after them,
as winds blow ships across the sea.

68 His mentality is stabilized
whenever one withdraws the sense
in every way and every side
from objects of his every sense.

69 When every being sleeps at night
   the man of discipline will wake,
   and for the seeing sage it is night
   when all the other beings wake.

70 The sea as waters enter it may fill
   forever yet its depths are always still,
   so he thro' whom all wishes flow arrives
   at peace, but not the man of sensual will.

On a higher note and longer metre, the disciplined mind is compared to the ocean, absorbing desires and not cherishing them

71 The man who abandons all desires
   in that his longing motions cease,
   who never thinks that 'I am this'
   or 'this is mine', proceeds to peace.

The notions of 'I' and 'mine' delude man and peace lies beyond them

72 This is the still state of Brahman,
   with this be no more stupefied,
   one goes to the Calm of Brahman
   if here on dying he abide.

Brahman, the divine being, the basis of existence, the All, here joined with Calm (*Nirvana*) as absolute peace

SO ENDS
THE SECOND CHAPTER
AND ITS NAME IS
the Yoga of Theory

3
Action

Arjuna said:

Is the life of the mind superior to action? Action is necessary, but discipline is needed to bring detachment from rewards

1 If my activity you find
inferior to the state of mind,
then why are you commanding me
to violent activity?

2 With words apparently confused
you seem to lead my mind astray,
so tell me one thing certainly
that I may gain the better way.

The Blessed Lord said:

There are two ways of spiritual exercise, Knowledge-Method and Action-Method (Karma-Yoga), see 2, 39

3 A twofold system has been told
throughout the earth by me of old,
for reasoners Knowledge-discipline,
for workers Action-discipline.

Ascetic renunciation of action by itself cannot free from the entail of action and bring perfection

4 A man by not beginning works
does not attain to worklessness,
nor simply by renouncing works
can he arrive at perfectness.

5 Nobody for the shortest time
remains without doing anything,
but each is made to act perforce
by the Qualities that from Nature spring.

Action comes from the Qualities or Strands of Nature, see 2, 45

6 And he is called a hypocrite
who just restrains his action-sense
but sits and ponders, foolish soul,
with thoughts upon the things of sense.

See 2, 59

7 For whosoever undertakes,
  with sense by intellect possessed,
  disciplined acts with action-sense
  yet is detached, he proves the best.

8 Since work is better than no work
  perform the action that you need,
  even the body's sustenance
  without some work will not succeed.

9 Except in sacrificial work
  the world is bound by activity,
  so for that purpose do your work
  but always from attachment free.

A short section, 9–16, considers the purpose of sacrifice and the origins of the world

10 When the Creator-god of old
   had fashioned men and rites he told
   his people: 'Create yourselves and now
   in this shall be your Wishing-Cow.'

A mythical cow granted all desires, but wishes are fulfilled by doing duty. Sacrifice pleases the gods and they help men in return

11 By this you benefit the gods
   so let the gods reward you too
   and supporting one another
   this highest good will come to you.

12 Prospered by your sacrifices
   the gods will give desired relief,
   but he who simply takes their gifts
   without return is just a thief.

13 Some good men eat ritual leavings
   and all their evil acts are gone,
   but the wicked ones eat evil
   by cooking for themselves alone.

Those who devour the remains of food given in sacrifice, see 4, 31

14 All beings are derived from food
   and food by raindrops germinates,
   rain itself depends on worship
   and worship from acts originates.

Brahman here may mean
Nature at first, and then
the Imperishable, the All,
see 2, 72

15 From the Imperishable comes Brahman
and out of Brahman works arise,
so the universal Brahman
is ever based on sacrifice.

In the wheel of Brahman
all subsists and with it one
must revolve or work

16 Thus the wheel was set in motion
and he who turns it not again
is evil, finding his delight
in sensual things and lives in vain.

17 But he who only loves the soul,
who is happy in the soul alone,
has nothing that he ought to do
contented in the soul alone.

He is not obliged to work,
but he acts in detachment

18 He has no aim in action done
on earth or action left undone,
no purpose where he might depend
on any being for any end.

19 Therefore be always unattached
when you do your necessary work,
man advances to the Highest
if he detached performs his work.

The example of a famous
king, father of Sita the
wife of the divine hero
Rama

20 King Janaka and others won
perfection by their actions done,
so do your action as you should
or just for universal good.

21 For as the noblest man behaves
so will all other people do,
and by the example that he sets
the world will always that pursue.

God has no obligation to
act and nothing to gain,
yet he works to sustain
the worlds

22 For me there is nothing to be done,
nothing is unattained to gain
of any kind in all three worlds
and yet at work I still remain.

23 If I should fail to persevere
   in all my work unwearying,
   people would follow on my path
   and copy me in everything.

24 And if I performed no action
   the worlds would come to end in void,
   I'd be an agent of confusion
   if all these creatures I destroyed.

25 Thoughtless people in doing work
   to every action stay attached,
   but to gain the welfare of the world
   the wise should act yet stay detached.

26 Then let him not confuse the mind
   of the ignorant who are attached to works,
   while they take pleasure in their tasks
   the wise man integrated works.

   His self is disciplined and integrated

27 Material Nature's Qualities
   are potent in all sorts of act,
   but the soul deluded by the ego
   imagines: 'It is I who act.'

   Man thinks that the soul
   is involved in action, but
   it is the Qualities of
   Nature that are at work,
   see 3, 5

28 So he who knows the real scope
   of actions and the Qualities
   remains detached and understands—
   'The Qualities act on the Qualities.'

29 Those who are bound to works of the
      Qualities
   are deluded by Nature's Qualities,
   but let not one who fully knows
   upset the dull who partly knows.

30 Put your mind on what concerns the soul,
   casting your actions on to me,
   throw off your fever, go and fight,
   from lust and egotism free.

   Thinking of what pertains
   to the self (see 7, 29) and
   relating actions to God

C

31 The ones who constantly pursue
    my doctrine, any men like these,
    not murmuring but full of faith
    from results of action find release.

32 Those who criticize my teaching
    and never try to practise it
    are deluded from all wisdom,
    completely lost and lacking wit.

33 Keeping to his proper Nature
    everyone acts, the wise man too,
    beings follow out their Nature
    whatever can repression do?

34 For all the senses concentrate
    on sensual objects lust and hate,
    yet one must not be ruled by these
    for they are both his enemies.

Do the duty of your own
nature and station,
see 18, 47

35 Far better do one's duty ill
    that do another's duty well,
    in one's own duty better die,
    in other's duty harm will lie.

Arjuna said:

Even when one perceives
and wills the good,
passions drive man to
evil, see 6, 34

36 Then by what influence impelled
    does any man commit a sin
    and even act against his will
    as driven by a force within?

The Blessed Lord said:

37 This derives from lust and anger
    springing from Passion's Quality,
    all-consuming, very wicked,
    perceive this as your enemy.

38 Compared with fire by smoke obscured
    or a mirror with dirt, just so
    a membrane hides the embryo
    and the world is by that lust obscured.

39 That everlasting enemy
    whose form is shaped by fierce desire
    obscures the wisdom of the wise
    and is a never sated fire.

40 The senses, brain and mind are places
    wherein it takes its stand, they say,
    and by those obscuring wisdom
    it leads the embodied soul astray.

41 Therefore you must at first begin
    to bring senses into discipline,
    thus smiting down this thing of ills
    that Pure and Practical Wisdom kills.

Lust will destroy both
theoretical and practical
wisdom, see 7, 2

42 The senses, so they say, are high,
    reason than senses yet more high,
    higher than reason is the mind
    and He is higher still than mind.

Above senses is the mind,
above mind is true being,
above that the Great Soul,
the Unmanifest and Eternal
Spirit, see Katha 3, 10; 6, 7

43 Know Him as higher than the mind
    and strengthen by yourself the soul,
    attack the foe that by its will
    is changing form and hard to find.

The enemy that has the
form of desire and is
hard to reach

SO ENDS
THE THIRD CHAPTER
AND ITS NAME IS
the Yoga of Action
(KARMA)

4
Wisdom

The Blessed Lord said:

The Method (Yoga) of
disciplined action is
eternal and was given to
sages of old. Vivasvat, the
sun, father of Manu the
first man. His son was
Ikshvaku

1 This is the Method I proclaimed
to Vivasvat and 'tis unchanged,
Vivasvat to Manu did unfold
what Manu to Ikshvaku told.

2 The royal sages knew of it
received successively in line
until this Method disappeared
from off the earth in course of time.

3 This ancient Method, just the same,
is what I now to you proclaim,
this is the highest mystery
for you my friend and devotee.

Arjuna said:

4 Vivasvat's birth was earlier
and later on your birth occurred,
that you proclaimed it at the first
how can I understand this word?

The Blessed Lord said:

5 Many a birth have I passed thro'
and many others came to you,
while everyone of these I know
yet by yourself you cannot know.

All beings have many lives
but only God understands
them, see 7, 26

Important verses declare
the bodily appearance of
the deity by creative power

6 My Self is changeless and unborn
and I am Lord of every being
but using Nature, which is mine,
by my own Power I come to being.

7 For whensoever Righteousness
   begins to fade away on earth,
   whenever grows Unrighteousness
   at once I send myself to birth.

When Right (*dharma*)
declines and Unright rises,
then the divinity appears
bodily

8 For the protection of the good,
   for Right to gain stability
   and for the wrong to be destroyed,
   age after age I come to be.

9 The man who knows my godly birth
   and understands my mode of deeds
   will never find another birth
   but after death to me proceeds.

10 Relieved of passion, fear and hate,
   with me their refuge, full of me,
   many have come to share my state
   made pure by wisdom's austerity.

11 However men draw near to me
   and wheresoever they may be
   'tis always in my path they go
   and I return their love just so.

God loves men in whatever
way they approach him,
see 7, 16 and 12, 14–20

12 The men who here adore the gods
   desire success from ritual deeds
   and quickly in the human world
   success from those same acts proceeds.

13 With appropriate Qualities and works
   the four-class system came from me,
   yet know that while I do all this
   I never act eternally.

Each of the four classes
has its proper actions:
priests, warriors,
merchants, servants,
see 18, 41

14 Since I seek no reward of works
   by works themselves am I not stained,
   and he who understands me thus
   by any work is not restrained.

God is at work but
unattached to rewards
and undefiled, see 3, 22

15 The ancient seekers of salvation
in knowing this their work have done,
and you must simply do your work
as ancients have of old begun.

What is the meaning of
work? Can it be
abandoned? No, it must
be performed in a detached
spirit and for no reward

16 What is action, what inaction?
this puzzles even sages still,
so I shall interpret action
and knowing it you are free from ill.

17 The course of action is obscure
so action must be understood
in its nature, with ill-action
and inaction also understood.

18 He who inaction in action
and act in no-act can realize,
does every action disciplined,
among his fellows he is wise.

19 One whose every undertaking
has neither motive nor desire
the wise declare a learnèd man
with works consumed in wisdom's fire.

20 Detached from all results of work,
independent and still content,
he really does no sort of work
altho' on work he goes intent.

21 Giving up all his possessions
not hoping, mind and soul restrained,
simply working with his body
and by defilement never stained.

Dualities, see 2, 45

22 Beyond the Dualities and greed,
content to take what chance has found,
the same in failure or success
tho' working he is never bound.

23 Released, and with attachment gone,
his mind is fixed in wisdom's sway,
he works for sacrifice alone
and all his action melts away.

Work is a form of
sacrifice, see 3, 9–15

24 The gift is Brahman, oil is Brahman,
by Brahman poured in Brahman-fire,
concentrated on work of Brahman
only to Brahman he'll aspire.

Brahman is everything,
sacrifice and the eternal,
and the man who works
goes to Brahman.
The same is said of
Krishna in 9, 16

25 Some adepts will devote themselves
to the gods alone with sacrifice,
some offer in the fire of Brahman
just sacrifice as sacrifice.

Other sacrifices are named
so as to extol knowledge

26 Some give in fires of self-restraint
their hearing and each other sense,
others offer sensual objects,
sounds and the like in fires of sense.

Ascetics who restrain
senses as by fire, and
those who let the senses
act on objects but are
detached

27 Others all the sensual actions
and workings of the breath commit
within the fire of self-control
whenever 'tis by wisdom lit.

Seekers after wisdom
control themselves and
actions

28 Some give austerity, some wealth,
some discipline and some again
give knowledge, or the Sacred Word,
as strictly vowed religious men.

29 Yet others offer inward breath
in outward breath, both out and in,
they check the flow both out and in,
intent upon control of breath.

Inward and outward
breath-control of some
kinds of meditation and
exercise

30 Some offer up control of breath,
and check their food in every way,
each understands the sacrifice
and thus their stains are done away.

31 They go to the eternal Brahman
who eat sweet ritual remains,
but one who never offers worship
not this world or the next attains.

All sacrifices and actions
are in the presence of the
Imperishable Brahman

32 So before the face of Brahman
these many kinds of worship go,
since all of them proceed from work
you find release when this you know.

33 But the sacrifice of wisdom
is better than wealth that men expend,
every work without exception
in wisdom finds its fullest end.

34 In reverence of the wise and service
and questioning your wisdom lies,
they alone will teach you wisdom
who see the truth and are really wise.

35 No more will you be led astray
if once you understand this way

The wise man sees the
basic identity of beings
and that all exist in God

and every being you shall see
within yourself and then in me.

36 Tho' among the evil-doers
there is no other creature worse

Cross the waters of evil
and rebirth in the boat of
wisdom, see 9, 30

simply in the ship of wisdom
this evil sea you shall traverse.

37 As a fire when it is kindled
reduces fuel into ash
even so the fire of wisdom
reduces actions into ash.

38 Nothing purifies like wisdom
and a man of perfect discipline,
since it is nowhere in the world
in time discovers this within.

39 So the man of faith gets wisdom,
   intent on this and sense restrains,
   then wisdom won to the highest peace
   before too long this man attains.

40 The ignorant, with doubting soul
   and lacking faith, will disappear,
   no bliss is for the doubting soul,
   no world beyond and nothing here.

41 Renouncing works by discipline,
   thro' wisdom all his doubts dispelled,
   one who is truly self-possessed
   by action can no more be held.

42 Your doubt, the child of ignorance,
   deep-rooted in your bosom lies,
   cleave it with the sword of wisdom,
   ruled by this Method, now arise!

SO ENDS
THE FOURTH CHAPTER
AND ITS NAME IS
the Yoga of Wisdom

5
Renunciation and Action

Arjuna said:

Renunciation of action is
different from disciplined
action (see 3, 1–8) but
they are not separate,
since a man of action
must also renounce desire
and rewards

1 You recommend renouncing acts
and also discipline of acts,
but which is better of the two?
Decisively tell me the facts.

The Blessed Lord said:

2 These both lead to the highest good,
renunciation, disciplined work,
but the discipline of actions
is better than renouncing work.

See 2, 45

3 One has full renunciation
when free from all Duality
he has no hatred or desire
and from the bonds of acts is free.

Earlier Reason was called
theory, but here it is
renunciation of binding
action, see 2, 39

4 Fools say Discipline and Reason
are different, but not the wise,
the man who fully uses one
the fruits of both will realize.

5 To the place attained by Reasoners
also the disciplined succeed,
and one who sees that Reason-method
is one with Discipline sees indeed.

Integration, the Yoga of
controlling and uniting,
by spiritual exercise

6 Lacking practised integration
renunciation is hard to gain,
disciplined in integration
the wise to Brahman soon attain.

7 The disciplined of pure soul
has self subdued and senses quelled,
his soul like every being's soul
and by activity not held.

See 4, 35

8 'I am really doing nothing'—
the integrated truly knows,
with sight and hearing, touch and smell,
he sleeps and breathes and eats and goes.

The soul is not engaged
in action of the senses,
see 3, 27

9 In opening or closing his eyes,
if he talk, or grasp, or evacuate,
he perceives that—'only the senses
on sensual objects operate.'

The senses move among
the things of sense

10 He abandons attachment when he works,
ascribing works to Brahman's powers
and stains of evil slip from him
as water slips from lotus flowers.

Water and mud slip off
lotus petals and leaves as
from an oiled surface

11 With body, mind and intelligence
and with the activities of sense,
the disciplined perform each deed
self-purified, attachment freed.

12 The integrated leaves results
of acts and lasting peace has gained,
the unintegrated act by lust
and by results of acts are chained.

13 In mind renouncing every work,
not working nor yet causing work,
in the Nine-gate city the embodied soul
sits happily, in full control.

The nine doors of the
body are mouth, ears,
eyes, nostrils, and lower
organs

14 The body's Lord no worldly work
nor power of activity creates,
nor joins the actions to results
but here his nature operates.

This lord is the individual
soul, see 15, 8

The soul does not begin
acts or receive results
tho' the ignorant think so

15 That Lord does not receive effects
of any good or evil deed,
wisdom obscured by ignorance
all creatures are by that deceived.

16 But if their wisdom overcome
that ignorance of self in some
their very wisdom, like the sun,
illuminates the Highest One.

That, the Highest, the
supreme Being

17 Their mind and soul are fixed on That,
That is their aim and That their way,
they take the path of no return
their stains by wisdom done away.

18 Even in a dog or outcaste
wise men perceive the same at least
as in a cow or elephant
or in a wise and courteous priest.

19 Already here they conquer birth,
their minds on that which stays the same,

Brahman is the same in all
beings, the wise men see
this and abide in it

therefore they abide in Brahman
for Brahman is faultless, still the same.

20 With steady mind and unconfused,
not pleased at gaining what he loves,
knowing Brahman, fixed in Brahman,
not grieved at having what he loathes.

21 He finds contentment in the soul
with self detached from outward ties,
he finds imperishable joy
controlled by Brahman-exercise.

22 Pleasures come from outward contacts
are nothing but a source of pain,
they have a beginning and an end
in which the wise discern no gain.

23 Only the man who here controls,
   before from the body he is free,
   the urges born of lust and wrath
   is integrated happily.

24 The disciplined has joy within
   and happiness and light within,
   therefore on becoming Brahman
   he will the Calm of Brahman win.

Become Brahman, immortal, in the Calm (*Nirvana*) of the All, see 2, 72

25 Their doubts dispelled in self-control
   the seers destroying every harm
   delight in the welfare of all beings
   and they attain to Brahman's Calm.

A popular phrase of general benevolence

26 These ones detached from lust and wrath,
   the holy men of thought-control
   will find the Calm of Brahman near
   since they are men who know the soul.

27 All outward contacts they despise
   fixing the gaze between the eyes,
   while evenly their breathing goes
   inwards and outwards thro' the nose.

Meditation, described more fully in 6, 10–15

28 The sage intent on full release
   controls the senses, reason, mind,
   is always thus and already saved
   leaves lust and fear and hate behind.

29 He knows *me* as the Recipient
   of worship and austerities,
   the Mighty Lord of all the World,
   Friend of all beings, and goes to peace.

Peace by the knowledge of God, object of worship and goal of life

SO ENDS
THE FIFTH CHAPTER
AND ITS NAME IS
*the Yoga of
Renunciation of Action*

6
Meditation

The Blessed Lord said:

The active life is the fulfilment of renunciation by disregarding rewards. The nature of the soul is discussed and then the practice of meditation

1 A man who does what must be done
unconcerned with results of work
at once renounces and yet acts
not those who have no rites or work.

2 What is called renunciation
you must know as action-discipline,
none without renouncing purpose
becomes possessed of discipline.

The first stage is action to gain control and then quietness to achieve integration

3 The sage who climbs to discipline
they say will take his acts as means,
for achieving integration
they claim tranquillity as means.

4 When to acts and sensual objects
he is not attached in any way
then renouncing every purpose
he climbs to discipline, they say.

Ambiguous verses. Soul or self (*atman*), used of lower and higher, particular and universal. A man should be uplifted by the Soul, or his own spiritual self

5 A man should raise the soul by the Soul
and never let the soul get low,
only the soul is friend of the Soul,
none but the soul is that Soul's foe.

6 The soul is friend towards that Soul
when soul is overcome by Soul,
deprived of the Soul hostility
the soul will show as enemy.

7 In one at peace and self-subdued
the Highest Soul absorbed remains,
the same in honour and disgrace,
in cold and heat and joy and pains.

Supreme Self, the soul is
absorbed or concentrated
in the Supreme

8 His self in theory and practice held,
immovable and sense-controlled,
the disciplined and integrated
alike finds clods and stones and gold.

See 14, 24

9 He is the best who has one mind
to neutral, ally, foe or friend,
indifferent to enemy or kin,
alike to good and evil men.

10 The disciplined who stays apart
seeks integration by control,
without possessions or desires,
alone, restraining thoughts and soul.

The practice of
meditation, 10-15,
requires solitude, bodily
and mental control, and
spirit fixed on God

11 Let him prepare himself a place
both clean and firm for sitting in,
not high or low and covered up
with sacred grass and cloth and skin.

12 Fixing the mind on one sole point
check thoughts and sense-activity,
sitting on the seat to practise
a disciplined self-purity.

13 With even body, neck and head,
steady and motionless one stays
while looking at the nose's end
not staring round in other ways.

See 5, 27

14 With tranquil soul and free from fear
abide in vows of chastity,
with thoughts on me, controlled in mind
and integrated, rapt in me.

The Lord is not only a
help to meditation but its
sole object

Self-discipline leads to
peace, the Calm of
Nirvana, which itself
subsists in God

15 With integration of himself
the disciplined with governed mind
the peace that culminates in Calm
and rests in me, will surely find.

16 Discipline is not for him who eats
too much or one who never eats,
neither for him who always sleeps
nor yet for one who never sleeps.

17 When food and pleasure are controlled,
when deeds and gestures one restrains,
when sleep and waking are controlled,
this integration scatters pains.

18 When thoughts are held in check and stilled
in the soul alone, whoever can
be freed from lust for all desires
is called an integrated man.

19 'As a lamp will never flicker
in a windless room'—this simile
shows the disciplined with thought controlled
is practising self-mastery.

20 Curbed by practised integration
when his thought returns to quietness
then by the self one sees the Soul
and finds in the Soul contentedness.

21 Beyond the senses, only grasped
by the mind is that continual bliss
and he who knows it never swerves
from truth, remaining fixed in this.

22 Achieving this he will consider
there cannot be a higher prize,
he firmly stands and is not moved
by any grievous miseries.

23 This breaking of the link with pain
    he understands as discipline,
    resolved with undespondent heart
    to practise constant discipline.

This state, disunion from union with pain, is Yogic discipline. A play on the meanings of union and yoking

24 Giving up without remainder
    all lusts that to the will belong,
    only by the mind restraining
    the whole of senses' busy throng.

25 Little by little he comes to rest,
    making his thought in the Soul abide,
    his mind held firm in steadiness
    and thinking of nothing else beside.

26 Whenever thoughts revolve around
    since they are flickering, unsound,
    in all such things one must control
    and subject them to obey the Soul.

27 Towards the man of tranquil mind
    the highest kind of blessing comes,
    the disciplined has passion stilled
    and stainless Brahman he becomes.

See 5, 24

28 Always integrating himself
    the disciplined is free from stains
    and easily into touch with Brahman
    and also highest bliss attains.

29 And when his self is disciplined
    he sees himself in every being
    and all the beings in himself
    who just the same in all is seeing.

Or the Soul in every being, see 4, 35

30 The man who sees me everywhere,
    discerning everything in me,
    I am not ever lost to him
    and he is never lost to me.

The same self is in all beings, and God is in all and will never lose his devotee

D

31 In unity and loving me
    as in all beings I abide,
    in whatsoever state they be
    the disciplined in me abide.

Because of the likeness of
selves he sees that joy and
sorrow in others are the
same as in himself

32 Comparing beings with himself
    in everything he sees the same,
    whether this is pain or pleasure
    and is most disciplined, men claim.

Arjuna said:

33 This discipline that you explain
    by treating everything the same,
    I feel has no stability
    because of man's inconstancy.

Not only the passions but
the mind struggles against
the truth and needs
discipline, see verse 26
and 3, 36

34 Impetuous, stubborn, violent
    and fickle is the human mind,
    I believe that to restrain it
    is hard as to confine the wind.

The Blessed Lord said:

35 It is true the mind is fickle
    and hardly any way controlled,
    yet by untiring exercise
    and practice it is yet controlled.

36 I think an unself-governed man
    finds integration hard to gain,
    the self-controlled by proper means
    and striving finds he can attain.

Arjuna said:

What about a man who
fails to keep to the
practice of disciplined
self-control?

37 But an unsuccessful man of faith
    whose thoughts have lapsed from discipline
    on what path will he go who fails
    full integration here to win?

38 To perish like a cloven cloud
   from both of these he falls away,
   with no foundation wandering
   perplexed along the Brahman way?

39 This difficulty of my doubt
   I beg you utterly dispel,
   because the answer to my doubt
   no other one but you can tell.

The Blessed Lord said:

40 A man like this is not destroyed
   in this world or the next, my friend,
   for nobody who acts aright
   can finish with an evil end.

41 He wins the worlds of virtuous men
   and there for countless years will dwell,
   then reborn to pure and noble folk
   this man whose discipline once fell.

One who has faith gains a heavenly reward and is then reborn on earth

42 Or else to learnèd families
   of the disciplined he comes again,
   tho' such a birth as that on earth
   is even harder to attain.

He is reborn to a better family and gets again on the path of self-control

43 And there he wins the unity
   he had with his mind in former lives,
   from the condition that he reached
   on to perfection still he strives.

The association that he had before is won again, and the effect of previous discipline bears him on

44 By the force of former practice
   he is borne along without his will,
   or one who simply seeks control
   transcends repeated ritual.

Discipline of self is more important than Word-Brahman or scripture repetition

45 The disciplined who fights with zeal
and purified from evil deeds,
perfected thro' his many births
upon the highest path proceeds.

See 3, 42 and 12, 12   46 The disciplined, above ascetics,
ranks better than the wise and can
rise higher than the man of works,
so be an integrated man.

47 Of the disciplined who are controlled
he is integrated most I hold
whose inner soul is absorbed in me
and with faith declares his love to me.

SO ENDS
THE SIXTH CHAPTER
AND ITS NAME IS
the Yoga of Meditation

7
Theoretical and Practical Wisdom

The Blessed Lord said:

1 If your mind is attached to me
be disciplined and rely on me
and listen how without a doubt
you will come to know me utterly.

The divine nature is
revealed in lower and
higher forms, though few
can understand it fully

2 I shall elucidate in full
Theoretical Wisdom and Practical,
you will know it in this world and so
nothing else will be left to know.

Practical experience is
deeper than theory, see
verses 8–12 where
experience of God is
expounded

3 Among the thousands of mankind
but one perfection seeks maybe,
and who perfection seek and find
maybe just one in truth knows me.

4 In earth and water, fire and wind,
space, mind and conscience, into eight,
adding the ego faculty,
so does my Nature separate.

The lower manifested
Nature is analysed into an
eightfold division; five
gross elements, with mind,
consciousness, and ego

5 Other than this one which is low
my higher Nature you must know,
that is the Life by which sustained
the universe is all maintained.

The higher divine Nature
is the very Life of the
universe, the power in
everything

6 All beings have their origin
in this, certainly that is true,
I am the source of the universe
and I am its dissolution too.

7   There is no other higher thing
    superior in life to me,
    this universe is strung on me
    just like a row of pearls on string.

These are the more
important manifestations
of the divine. Others are
listed in 10, 20–40

Sacred Word, OM, the
sacred syllable of the
Upanishads, see 8, 13

8   I am the Flavour in the water,
    in moon and sun am I as Light,
    the sacred Word in all the Vedas,
    the Sound in space and manhood's Might.

9   I am the Fragrance in the earth,
    the Flames that in the fire appear,
    I am the Life in every being,
    Austerity in men austere.

10 I am the Seed of every being,
    the Eternal, know assuredly,
    I am the Mind of the enlightened,
    I am Glory in the majesty.

Desire or love, where it
is not inconsistent with
right

The three Qualities or
Strands of Nature (see
2, 45) all come from the
divine nature, though
men are deluded by them

11 I am the Power of the mighty
    when freed from lust and longing's fire,
    and where the law has not forbidden
    within the creatures I'm desire.

12 Whatever states derive from Goodness
    you know they only come from me,
    as of Passion or of Darkness,
    I am not in them but they're in me.

13 By these three states of Qualities
    this universe is led astray
    and all have failed to recognize
    I am changeless, greater far than they.

14 For this is my celestial Power
    in the Qualities and hardly passed,
    yet those who trust in me alone
    beyond this Power go at last.

15 But deluded evil-doers
   come not to me, such evil men
   robbed of wisdom by delusion
   return to demon-states again.

As God's devotees turn
to his being, so evil men
turn to that of demons

16 Four kinds of people worship me
   as virtuous folk—those who desire
   some private gain, the suffering,
   the wise who know, or who inquire.

Four types: followers of
legitimate wealth, the
distressed, those who seek
wisdom, and those who
possess it

17 The wise man who loves the One excels
   and in constant integration dwells,
   to the wise man I am very dear
   and he himself to me is dear.

The man who loves the
one Lord, or is of single
devotion, is dear to God.
See 4, 11 and 12, 14–20

18 All these are noble but the wise
   I consider as my very soul,
   with integrated self he comes
   to me alone as highest goal.

19 And at the end of many a birth
   the wise who is to me resigned
   will think that 'Vasudeva is all',
   yet such a Great Soul is hard to find.

Vasudeva, a name of
Krishna, the wise man
knows that all beings
subsist in him

20 Driven on by their own Nature,
   deprived of wisdom by many a lust,
   adopting various religious rules,
   some men in other gods may trust.

21 To this or that form devotees
   present their worship having faith,
   yet I myself will allocate
   to everyone unswerving faith.

Men may worship many
gods but their faith comes
from the one God

22 And disciplined with such a faith,
   when seeking his desires to gain
   whatever he propitiate
   that is what I myself ordain.

23 Yet results are small and definite
   for men who have such little wit,
   to the gods they go if gods they please
   but to me resort my devotees.

Ignorant critics think the
Lord's revealed form is all
there is, see 9, 11

24 Unmanifest, and now manifest,
   thus foolish men of me may deem,
   not knowing that my higher state
   remains Unchanging and Supreme.

25 To all men I am not revealed
   by my creative Power concealed,
   the deluded world perceives me not,
   the Unborn and one that Changes Not.

See 4, 5

26 I know the beings that are past
   and beings that are yet to be
   and everyone of present time
   but nonetheless not one knows me.

The Dualities, Pairs of
opposites, bind men to
confusion, but by
integration of personality
this duality can be
overcome see 2, 45

27 Delusion from Dualities
   confuses every being on earth
   arising from desire and hate
   beginning at the time of birth.

28 But those whose wrong has come to end,
   the men of meritorious deed,
   love me with steadfast promises
   and from the confusing Pairs are free.

Brahman and Karma in
their wholeness will be
dealt with in the next
chapter, and what has
reference to the soul or
self

29 The man who strives and on me relies,
   released in age and when he dies,
   will know of Brahman as a whole
   and all Works, and what concerns the soul.

30 The ones who know concerning me
in beings, gods and worship, find
that at the hour of passing on
they know with integrated mind.

Concerning beings,
divinity, sacrifice. These
terms are sometimes
translated as Over-being,
Essential Self, etc., but
they are common in the
Upanishads as referring to
the self, etc. Brihad-
aranyaka Upanishad
5, 14, 4, etc.

SO ENDS
THE SEVENTH CHAPTER
AND ITS NAME IS

the Yoga of
Theoretical and
Practical Wisdom

8
The Imperishable Brahman

Arjuna said:

The words at the end of the last chapter are expounded briefly, ending with fixing thoughts on God

1 What's that Brahman? what concerns the
   soul?
   what are Works? and how do men define
   whatever appertains to beings?
   what appertains to things divine?

2 What is there concerning worship
   in this body, how proves it so?
   and how yourself at time of death
   may men of governed spirit know?

The Blessed Lord said:

The Imperishable is a name for the supreme principle Brahman, active in the perishable world which produces Works (*karma*)

So far as it regards the gods it is the cosmic Spirit

Krishna is here identified with sacrifice, see 9, 16

3 The Imperishable is highest Brahman,
   'tis inborn nature for the soul,
   as that which causes states of beings
   'tis Karma which creates the whole.

4 In beings it is their perishable state,
   but Spirit in divinity,
   and when this relates to worship
   here in the body that is me.

5 Whoever at the time of death
   on me alone can meditate
   shall leave the body when he dies
   and surely go to my estate.

The dying man is conformed to or growing into the condition of the being worshipped

6 Whatever state he bears in mind
   at death and leaves his frame aside
   to that very state he will arrive
   and ever after there abide.

7   Therefore you must proceed to strive
    but every moment think of me,
    fixing on me your mind and thoughts
    not doubting you will come to me.

8   If disciplined practice integrates
    one's mind which never deviates
    to that divine and highest Spirit
    one goes and on him meditates.

9   The Ancient Seer this Governor they call,
    unthinkable in form, smaller than the small,
    who meditates on him, beyond the dark
    sun-coloured and Establisher of all,

Long metre. That supreme
Spirit sun-coloured beyond
the darkness;
Shvetashvatara Upanishad
3, 8
Smaller than the small,
greater than the great,
Katha 2, 20

10 With mind unmoving at the departure time
    devotion and controlling power confine,
    forcing the breath between the eyebrow space
    one finds the Spirit, highest and divine.

A brief reference to
breath control, see verse
12, and 5, 27

11 The Imperishable which Veda-knowers meant
    ascetics follow with all passion spent,
    desiring this men live in chastity,
    to show this state in brief is my intent.

The word which all the
Vedas rehearse, all
austerities proclaim, for
which men live religiously,
that I briefly tell you;
Katha 2, 15

12 Closing all the bodily doors
    confine your mind within the heart,
    retain the breath within the head
    to practised concentration start.

See 5, 13

13 Remember me and utter OM
    Brahman the Imperishable in one,
    who does this and leaves the body
    upon the highest way has gone.

The sacred word,
Brahman, in one syllable,
see 7, 8

14 Thinking of me incessantly
    the constant man of discipline
    with mind on nothing else at all
    discovers I am not hard to win.

15 Having gained supreme perfection
the great-souled men who come to me
never find reincarnation
that transient home of misery.

Brahma, a personal god of
heavenly worlds; all
worlds are subject to
recurrent existence

16 The worlds as far as Brahma's realm
dissolve and then return around,
but everyone who comes to me
has no more transmigration found.

17 Such men know the Days of Brahma
will each a thousand ages last,
and each Night a thousand ages,
and know how Day and Night are passed.

The Unmanifest is Nature
or primal matter, which is
originally and finally
unknown but produces
manifested things, see 9, 8

18 All manifested things spring out
at Day from the Unmanifest
and then dissolve again at Night
in that same one Unmanifest.

19 That whole company of beings
over and over must appear,
helplessly dissolve at nightfall
and rise again when Day is near.

Beyond unmanifest
Nature, which comes to
manifestation, is the
unmanifest God

20 But a higher mode of being
when every being is wholly void,
Unmanifest beyond the Unmanifest,
is primal and is not destroyed.

21 Unmanifest, Imperishable,
men say that is the highest road
and once attained there is no return
since that is my supreme Abode.

The Supreme Being is
won only by love (*bhakti*)

22 This then is the highest Spirit
whom love alone appropriates,
all lesser beings held in him
the universe he permeates.

23 Now I will inform you of the times
    at which the disciplined return
    from over there when they have gone
    and then the times of non-return.

24 In six months of the sun's north way,
    in fire, light, day, bright moon, why then
    those who die ascend to Brahman
    for they are Brahman-knowing men.

These verses reflect
primitive thought. Those
who die in the north
course of the sun and
bright half of the moon
pass to cremation fire, go
to Brahma and do not
return. Those who die in
the dark and southern
period pass into cremation
smoke, go to the moon
and are reborn. Brihad-
aranyaka Upanishad 6, 2,
15

25 The six months of the sun's south way,
    in smoke and night, dark moon, are when
    the disciplined attains the moon
    but from its light comes back again.

26 These paths of light and dark they hold
    are everlasting for the world,
    by one man goes to no return,
    by the other to a sure return.

27 If he knows of these two courses
    no disciplined man is fooled therein,
    so be always integrated
    by means of steady discipline.

28 Whatever fruit of merit they ordain
    in scriptures, rituals, alms, ascetic pain,
    the disciplined knows this, surpassing all
    and will the highest primal state attain.

Long metre
By integration of self one
goes far beyond rituals to
the primal sphere. See
11, 48

SO ENDS
THE EIGHTH CHAPTER
AND ITS NAME IS
*the Yoga of
the Imperishable Brahman*

9
Royal Knowledge and Royal Mystery

The Blessed Lord said:

The praise of the divine being in all things, by power creating and upholding the universe

1 Since you have uttered no objections
a greater mystery I'll reveal,
of Practical and Theory Wisdom
and knowing it you're free from ill.

2 This is the highest purifier,
royal wisdom, royal mystery,
most quickly comprehensible,
unchanging yet done easily.

3 The men who exercise no faith
nor hold to this religious truth
cannot attain me but are bound
upon the endless dying round.

See 8, 15

4 All this cosmos is pervaded
by me in form Unmanifest.
In me all beings must subsist
altho' in them I never rest.

They exist in God as their Inner Controller but his existence does not depend on them

5 Yet beings do not rest in me,
behold my sovereign activity!
Support of beings yet not in beings
is my Self that causes things to be.

6 The mighty wind is always blowing
in space and all can penetrate,
and even so does every being
abide in me, be sure of that.

7 Back to my material Nature
all kinds of beings flow, from when
a period ends and when a period
begins I send them forth again.

See 8, 18

8 I despatch by my own Nature,
again and ever issuing
in the power of my Nature,
all this helpless host of being.

Beings are produced by
God consorting with or
subduing Nature, see 14, 3

9 And yet I am not bound at all
in any manner by these works,
but sit as one indifferent
and stay detached among these works.

Indifferent, sitting in as
sitting out, the divine
detachment, see 14, 23

10 For Nature while I supervise
makes moving and unmoving being,
and as this motive-power applies
the universe is orbiting.

11 Some foolish people may despise
my taking of a human guise,
ignoring that my higher state
is Lord of Beings, that most great.

The divine appearance in
human form from age to
age (see 4, 7) may be
scorned by those who
know nothing of his
unmanifested essence,
see 7, 24

12 Vain in hopes and vain in actions,
void of knowledge and wit are they,
dwelling in a monstrous nature
of demons and which leads astray.

13 But those who dwell in godlike nature
and know me are men of Mighty Soul,
they love me with unswerving thoughts
as Source of Beings, Unchangeable.

14 They glorify me constantly
with eager zeal and steadfast vow
and integrated pay me homage
as in their love to me they bow.

15 With wisdom as a sacrifice
   others to me such worship pay
   in my unique and many forms,
   as various, facing every way.

Krishna identifies himself
with sacrifice (8, 4), and
so with Brahman (see
4, 24), linking this world
and the eternal
The oil is the sacred
butter of sacrificial fire,
the verse (*mantra*) is the
sacred formula

OM, see 8, 13

16 I am the rite, the sacrifice,
   the herb, the gift towards the dead,
   I am the fire, the oblation poured,
   I am the oil, the verse that's said.

17 I am the Father of this world,
   the Purifier, what is known,
   Mother, Grandsire and the Founder,
   the first three Vedas, sacred OM.

18 Goal, Sustainer, Lord and Witness,
   the Home and Friend, Resort in need,
   the Dissolution, Source and Basis,
   the Treasure-house and changeless Seed.

19 I give the heat and I restrain
   at first and then send out the rain,
   both Being and Non-being am I,
   both Death and Immortality.

Long metre
Users of old rites and
texts

20 The ritual-drinkers offer sacrifice,
   believe three Vedas, seek for paradise,
   and cleansed from faults they win pure godly
       worlds
   and taste the gods' enjoyments in the skies.

They reach heaven but
return to earth. Men who
want desires win only the
state of rebirth

21 But when they have enjoyed wide heaven's
       domain
   their merit spent the mortal world they gain,
   so those who hold too fast the threefold law
   and long for lust will come and go again.

22 But to those who think of me alone,
   who serve me and who persevere,
   I bring the power to attain
   and guard what they have gathered here.

23 Some with faith may offer worship
   to other gods as devotees
   but that is only me they worship
   tho' not in ways the law decrees.

See 7, 21–2

24 I am Recipient and Lord
   of sacrifices one and all,
   those who do not recognize me
   and see the truth are sure to fall.

See 5, 29

They will return to this
world if they do not know
God truly

25 Their worshippers attain the gods,
   to ancestors go each votary,
   ghost-worshippers attain the ghosts,
   and those who serve me come to me.

26 A leaf or flower, fruit or water
   a man in love to me may bring,
   and from that zealous soul I relish
   what love presents in offering.

A favourite verse of
simple devotion of love
(*bhakti*)

27 In what you do and what you eat,
   in offerings that you present,
   in all austerities performed
   be evermore on me intent.

28 Thus released from bonds of action
   good or bad fruits, in discipline
   by practice and renunciation
   your soul is free and me you win.

29 I am the same towards all beings,
   none is disliked or dear to me,
   they are in me and I am in them
   who worship me by loving me.

E

30 Even a very evil-doer
    who just loves me with all his might
    must be reckoned with the righteous,
    his resolution being right.

31 Very soon his soul is righteous
    and he attains eternal peace,
    none of my devotees are lost
    and you can be assured of this.

The religion of love is
open to all classes, those
of mixed caste, merchants,
women, and the lowest
ranks

32 All who come to me for refuge
    including those whose birth is low,
    artisans and women, even serfs,
    upon the highest path shall go.

33 But how much better virtuous priests
    and loving royal seers must be!
    You gained this passing joyless world
    so now devote yourself to me.

34 Pay me homage, give me worship,
    on me your love, on me your mind,
    with integrated soul in me
    and surely me alone you find.

SO ENDS
THE NINTH CHAPTER
AND ITS NAME IS
*the Yoga of
Royal Wisdom and Royal Mystery*

10
Pervading Power

The Blessed Lord said:

1 Now as a higher message yet
   listen to this that I shall tell
   both because you delight in it
   and also that I wish you well.

The Supreme Being is the source of gods and sages, and wise men should revere him as the origin of all. His mystical powers are now revealed pervading the universe

2 The mighty seers and hosts of gods
   know nothing of my origin,
   I am the beginning of the gods
   and mighty seers in everything.

3 He who knows me, Great Lord of Worlds,
   the Unborn and the Beginningless,
   he of undeluded mortals
   from every evil finds release.

4 From me alone all states of beings
   derive in their diversities;
   in mind and wisdom, non-delusion,
   in patience, truth, control and peace,

Parts of verses 4–5 are reversed to introduce the states that come from God

5 In pleasure, pain, existing, dying,
   in fear or safety, harmlessness,
   in contentment, fame or infamy,
   in austerity or bounteousness.

6 The seven mighty seers of old
   and the Manus four from me arose,
   all were the offspring of my mind
   and worldly creatures spring from those.

Four Manus ruled the four world ages, see 4, 1

The far-flung power or
supernal manifestation of
the deity, illustrated in the
following verses

7 Whoever knows my Pervading Powers
and energies which work therein
is integrated certainly
in undivided discipline.

8 I am the Origin of all,
from me all creatures emanate
the wise know this and give me love
as thoroughly affectionate.

9 With thoughts and life absorbed in me
they offer one another light
and talking of me constantly
they find content and true delight.

10 To those men always disciplined
who evermore show love to me
I give that integrated mind
by means of which they come to me.

11 Their darkness born of ignorance
in kindliness I dissipate
by the shining lamp of wisdom
and yet remain in my own state.

Arjuna said:

The Supreme Deity is
beyond the gods and the
neuter Brahman, see 11, 37

12 Highest Brahman, Highest Dwelling
Eternal Spirit, Primal God,
You Purifier all-excelling,
Divine, Unborn, Pervading Lord.

Famous sages, Vyasa the
author of the Gita

13 So all sages have proclaimed you
with Narada the heavenly seer,
Vyasa, Asita, Devala,
and thus you yourself to me declare.

14 For everything you say to me,
   O Master, I believe is so
   and yet your manifested state
   neither the gods nor demons know.

The way in which God is
manifested in human form
and shows his power on
earth

15 You only comprehend yourself
   as Highest Spirit by yourself,
   the Lord of Beings, beings' source,
   God of gods, Lord of the universe.

16 But those divine Pervading Powers
   declare conclusively I pray,
   of your own self as you pervade
   the worlds and yet forever stay.

Immanent in the worlds
and yet unchanged

17 How may I know you, Lord of Power,
   forever on you pondering?
   How may you be conceived by me
   and in what various states of being?

18 In fullest detail tell me more
   your Method and Pervading Power,
   I've not enough since I have heard
   the nectar of your deathless word.

The Blessed Lord said:

19 Come then, I will explain to you
   at least the chief ones which transcend
   of my divine Pervading Powers,
   because unbounded I extend.

20 In the heart of every being
   I am the Soul installed to dwell,
   the Origin and Midst of beings
   I also am their End as well.

The divine Pervading
Powers are revealed in the
chief of all classes of beings
and states

Vishnu the chief of the
heavenly deities, and
Marichi chief of Maruts
of storms

21 I am Vishnu of the sky gods,
   the radiant Sun among the lights,
   I am Marichi of the storm gods,
   I am the Moon of stars at nights.

Indra first of the Vedic
gods and Sama, the
chanted, of the three
Vedas

22 I am Indra among the deities,
   the Sama of the Vedas taught,
   I am Mind among the senses
   and among the beings I am Thought.

Shiva, both kindly and
terrible
Meru, a mythical
mountain in the middle
of the world

23 I am Shiva of destroyers,
   the Lord of Wealth of sprites and freaks,
   I am Fire among the brilliant
   and Meru of the mountain-peaks.

24 I am the chief among the priests,
   their god Brihaspati is me,
   I am the God of War of captains,
   among the waters I'm the Sea.

A Vedic seer
The syllable is OM,
see 7, 8

25 I am Bhrigu of great sages,
   of words the single Syllable,
   I am the murmured Prayer of worship,
   Himalaya of things immovable.

Pipal or Bo-tree, see 15, 1

26 The sacred Fig of all the trees
   and Narada of seers divine,
   Chitra-ratha of musicians,
   wise Kapila of perfect line.

Musicians, Gandharvas.
Kapila, reputed founder
of Samkhya teaching

Figures from the myths of
Indra and the gods

27 Indra's steed among the horses
   from Nectar of the sea I spring,
   as Indra's mount of elephants
   of human beings I am King.

See 3, 10

28 Of cows I am the Cow-of-wishes,
   of weapons the Thunderbolt that shakes
   I am the God of Love creating
   and I am the Serpent King of snakes.

29 The Endless of the fabled serpents,
the Water-god of water-beings,
the Senior of the ancestors
and I am Death the all-decreeing.

30 I am Prahlada of the demons
and I am Time of reckoning,
I am Vishnu's Mount among the birds
and of the animals I am King.

Virtuous son of a demon
king

31 I am Ganges of the rivers,
I am the Wind of purifiers,
Leviathan of water-monsters,
I am Rama of the warriors.

A hero and Avatar of
Vishnu

32 The Beginning of creations
I am the End and Middle too,
of sciences the Science of the Soul,
in disputation I am True.

33 I am the letter A of letters
and of compounded words the Pair,
I truly am immortal Time,
the Ordainer facing everywhere.

Paired or joined names

34 I am Death that carries all away,
the Origin of things to be,
and female nouns: Fame, Wisdom, Speech,
Luck, Firmness, Patience, Memory.

35 I am the Gayatri of metres,
the Greatest Chant of those men sing,
I am the First amid the months
and of the seasons I am Spring.

Metre of famous Vedic
verses

36 I am Conquest, Resolution,
the Dice of those who speculate,
I am the Goodness in the good,
I am the Greatness in the great.

Krishna's name and clan
Krishna is his hearer

37 I am Vasudeva of Vrishnis,
   you Arjuna of Pandu's sons,
   I am Vyasa of the hermits,
   wise Ushanas of thoughtful ones.

38 I am the Craft of would-be rulers,
   I am the Rod when men chastise,
   I am the Silence of the secret,
   I am the Wisdom in the wise.

39 I am whatever is the Seed
   in every other kind of being,
   without me nothing could exist,
   not one unmoved or moving being.

40 So my divine Pervading Powers
   as I have said can never end,
   in these examples I declared
   how my Pervading Powers extend.

41 Whatever shows Pervading Powers
   in either majesty or might
   be sure it springs in every case
   from just a part of my own light.

42 Yet what's the use for you to know
   so much of this extensive flow?

The universe is supported
with a fragment of the
divine being which abides
unchanged

   since all the cosmos I sustain
   with part of me yet full remain.

SO ENDS
THE TENTH CHAPTER
AND ITS NAME IS
*the Yoga of
Pervading Power*

11
The Vision of the Cosmic Form

Arjuna said:

1   In gracious favour you revealed
these words of highest mystery
relating what concerns the Soul
and banished my perplexity.

2   The origin and dissolution
of beings I have heard in full
by the detail which you have explained
and your Great Self unchangeable.

3   Just so it is as by your word
you told me this, O Highest Lord,
and yet I long to see your form,
the Greatest Spirit shown as God.

4   As Lord of Power please reveal
your very Self unchangeable
if you consider it can be
in any way discerned by me.

The Blessed Lord said:

5   By their hundreds and their thousands
you see my complex forms displayed,
celestial of various kinds
yet different in shape and shade.

6   The spirits of the Sun and Light,
Destruction, Storm and many more
with the pair of heavenly Horsemen
are marvels never seen before.

The Vision of the Divine
Being, verses 15–50, is the
most tremendous vision in
religious literature Beyond
the immanent divine
powers appears the
transcendent divine Form

There are countless divine
forms of many kinds

7   Behold the total universe
    in my body gathered into one
    with moving and unmoving things
    and all you want to see is done.

Arjuna is given a divine
eye for the vision

8   But since with your own natural eye
    you cannot see me on your own,
    I'll give you a celestial eye
    and so as God my power is shown.

The charioteer describes
Krishna's transfiguration
as Vishnu, Hari

Samjaya said:

9   Having spoken in this manner
    Hari, the mighty Yoga-Lord,
    made manifest to Arjuna
    his highest sovereign form as God.

10 This form had countless wondrous views

With symbols of all the
gods

    with heavenly ornaments and hues,
    had many a mouth and many an eye
    and heavenly weapons lifted high.

11 Garlands and wondrous robes he wore
    and wondrous scents and ointments bore,
    this God with marvellous display
    was endless and faced every way.

12 If ever in the sky there comes
    the splendour of a thousand suns
    that might resemble as a whole
    the splendour of that Mighty Soul.

13 In the body of the God of gods
    Arjuna together could behold
    the universe converged in one
    and yet divided many-fold.

14 Then Arjuna in astonishment
with hair erect, was full of dread,
bowing his head towards the God
folding his hands and thus he said:

Arjuna said:

15 O God, I see within that form of thine
all Deities and hosts of beings shine,
Brahma the Lord upon the lotus-throne
and all the seers along with snakes divine.

At the highest level of the whole poem, verses 15–50 are in longer metre and describe the transfigured deity
Brahma, a creator who rose from the body of Vishnu in a lotus

16 With mouths and eyes, arms, bellies manifold
I see thy endless form all this enfold,
no origin or midst or end of thee
in Every Form, All-Lord, can I behold!

17 Thy crown and mace and disc I faintly see
bewildered by the mass of brilliancy
that shines on every side and like the sun
in glory flames as fire immeasurably.

The colossal form of Vishnu bearing his arms and emblems

18 Thou art Imperishable, the highest theme
of wisdom, cosmic resting-place supreme,
thou changeless Guardian of eternal Law,
the everlasting Spirit, thee I deem.

19 Without beginning, midst or end, thy might
is endless and thine arms are infinite,
thine eyes are sun and moon, thy flaming mouth
with burning radiance sets the world alight.

20 Between the earth and sky on every side
by thee alone this space is occupied
and gazing at thy wondrous fearful forms,
O Mighty Soul, the worlds are terrified!

All beings are engulfed in
the divine: gods, sages,
nature spirits, ancestors,
demons, and men

21 Now into thee approach those gods in throng
and some bow lowly down afraid of wrong,
while hosts of mighty seers and perfect ones
cry 'Hail' and praise thee with abundant song.

22 Spirits of storm and sun and sky and rays,
all-gods, winds, horsemen and the fathers
gaze,
and minstrels, goblins, demons, perfect ones
are scanning thee who dost them all amaze.

23 Thy mighty form with many a mouth and eye,
O Mighty-armed, all arms and feet and thigh,
with many bellies, grim with many teeth,
the worlds see this and quake—and so do I!

24 Sky-touching, many colours incandesce,
great gaping mouths, huge eyes of fieriness,
O Vishnu, seeing thee my inner soul
is shaken, lacking peace and steadiness.

25 And when I glance towards thy mouths of
fire
with jagged tusks like dissolution's pyre
I find no way of refuge, Lord of gods,
be merciful, thou home of worlds entire!

The heroes of the battle-
field are absorbed into the
divine body at the fire of
world-dissolution

26 To thee go yonder Dhrita-rashtra's sons
together with their royal battalions,
where Bhishma, Drona, Karna marching on
accompany our own great champions.

27 Within thy yawning mouths they quickly
rushed
by horrid tusks in terror they were brushed
and some there are who caught between the
teeth
are visible to me with faces crushed.

28 As many flooded rivers breaking free
   rush quickly down towards the one great sea,
   so charged the heroes of the human world
   towards thy flaming mouths to enter thee.

29 As moths fly hurtling with a rapid aim
   to meet destruction in a burning flame,
   so all the worlds with rapid aim drew near
   and in thy mouths to their destruction came.

30 And licking up the worlds on every side
   devouring all in jaws that blazen wide,
   O Vishnu, how thy dreadful splendours burn
   throughout the cosmos which is glorified!

31 Of awful form, instruct me, who art thou?
   O Best of Gods, have mercy as I bow,
   I long to understand thee, Primal One,
   not comprehending thy procedure now.

Who is this Lord and
what is he doing with
warriors destroyed in
his mouth?

The Blessed Lord said:

32 Lo, I am Time, the cause of world decay,
   matured, resolved the worlds to take away,
   without your action all will cease to be,
   those soldiers standing in opposed array.

He is Time, Doom, or
Death, at the end of the
world-cycle

Even if Arjuna does not
fight the dissolution is in
process

33 And so arise to triumph wonderful,
   defeat your foes, enjoy a prosperous rule,
   for all these men were slain by me long since
   and you will only be the working tool.

The instrument of divine
action

34 Yon Drona, Bhishma, Jayadratha slay,
   Karna and other men of war today,
   they're slain by me already, waver not,
   now fight and beat your rivals in the fray.

Samjaya said:

35 Then folding hands and trembling at this
          word,

the Diademed, from Krishna having heard
his homage made, again to Krishna spoke,
bowed down and stammered being greatly
          stirred.

Arjuna said:

36 O Krishna, it is right that at thy praise
the world rejoices, glad in all its ways,
the monsters fly in fear to every part
and all the perfect host its homage pays.

37 O Mighty Soul, why should they not adore?
Greater than Brahman, First Progenitor,
Infinite Lord of Gods and world abode,
Imperishable, Being, Non-being—and yet
          more!

38 Thou art the Primal God, the Ancient Soul,
the highest Rest of universal whole,
the Knower and the Known, thy endless form
pervades the universe, its highest Goal.

39 As Wind and Death, as Water, Fire, so thee
as Moon, Creator, Ancestor, I see.
All hail! And homage be a thousandfold,
to thee All hail, and homage ever be!

40 All hail to thee, in front and from behind,
thou All! to thee be homage unconfined.
O thou of endless strength, unmeasured
          might,
fulfilling all, the All in thee I find.

41 And if I rashly thought of thee as friend,
   said 'Krishna, Yadav', Comrade', without
      end
   and unaware of thine own majesty
   thro' negligence or lovingness offend;

Arjuna fears that he has been too familiar with the embodied deity and asks forgiveness

42 Or if I showed thee disrespect in jest,
   at play or sitting, eating or at rest,
   sometimes alone or sometimes publicly,
   Unshaken Lord, forgive at my request!

43 Thou Father of the world, of motionless
   or moving things, dear Teacher whom we
      bless,
   in all the worlds no other equals thee,
   none greater, unexcelled in mightiness.

44 And to my prostrate body bending low,
   O Lord adorable, thy grace bestow,
   as father bears with son, as friend with
      friend,
   as lover with beloved, God s mercy show!

45 Things that were not revealed before I see,
   my heart is thrilled yet trembles fearfully,
   show me, O God, that other form of thine,
   O Lord of Gods, World Home, forbear with
      me!

46 With crown and mace and discus that you
      bore
   I long to see you present as before,
   O thousand-armed, of universal form,
   reveal your shape and with your arms just
      four!

The vision is so fearful that Arjuna pleads for a return to Krishna's human form

The Blessed Lord said:

47 Because of grace towards you I have shown
   this highest form by power of my own
   of splendour, universal, endless, prime,
   which none before but you has ever known.

The vision comes by
grace and is not merited
by ritual or asceticism

48 Not by the Vedas, sacrifice or fee,
   by study, rites or grim austerity,
   can I be seen within the world of men
   in such a form that you alone could see.

49 Have no alarm and dissipate your fear,
   be not perplexed and let your heart take
      cheer,
   for having seen this awful form of mine
   again behold my other form—right here!

Samjaya said:

50 When Vasudeva had declared the whole
   the frightened Arjuna he would console
   and taking once again his natural form
   assumed his gracious shape, the Mighty
      Soul.

Arjuna said:

The vision fades and in
short metre the disciple
speaks calmly

51 Now that your gracious human form
   once more I calmly contemplate
   I have mastered all my senses
   returning to their normal state.

The Blessed Lord said:

52 This form of mine which you observed
   is very difficult to see,
   this is the form that even gods
   desire in vision constantly.

53 However not as you behold
   can I be seen in such a guise
   by austerity or Vedas,
   by gifts of alms or sacrifice.

54 Only by undivided love
   can I in reality be seen
   in such a guise as you perceived
   and both be known and entered in.

Not formal rites but love
(*bhakti*) alone can give the
knowledge of God and
union with him

55 So work for me, intent on me,
   be free from ties, have love for me
   and lacking hate, whoever is so
   to everyone to me shall go.

SO ENDS
THE ELEVENTH CHAPTER
AND ITS NAME IS
the Yoga of
the Vision of Cosmic Form

F

12
Loving Devotion

Arjuna said:

Some worship God with loving devotion (*bhakti*) and others seek the Unmanifested Absolute by knowledge and austerity

1 The ever-integrated come
to worship you in love, while some
the Imperishable, Unmanifest,
but which know discipline the best?

The Blessed Lord said:

2 The men who fix their minds on me
and serve with constant discipline,
pervaded with the highest faith,
I hold are best in discipline.

3 But those who serve the Unmanifest,
the Imperishable and Undefined,
the Inconceivable, Unmoving,
the constant, firm and unconfined,

4 Equal-minded alike to all
the crowd of senses they restrain
rejoicing in the good of all,
these also only me attain.

To seek the abstract being by knowledge is hard, the way of love to God is speedy

5 And yet their toil is weightiest
whose thoughts pursue the Unmanifest,
for hardly can the embodied soul
attain the unmanifested goal.

6 But those who cast their works on me
in everything and firmly wait
with undivided discipline
revere me as they meditate.

7 And if their thoughts are fixed on me
    immediately I am found
    their Saviour from the mortal sea
    that forms this transmigrating round.

The Lord of grace saves
his devotees from the cycle
of death and redeath

8 Arouse your soul to enter me
    and fix your mind on me alone
    as never doubting that henceforth
    you'll truly find in me your home.

9 If you are not able steadfastly
    to concentrate your thoughts on me
    then seek me as you realize
    the discipline of exercise.

Exercise, practice, with-
drawing of thought and
fixing it again and again
on an object

10 If you lack strength for exercise
    then make your aim work for my sake,
    and if you simply act for me
    then as result perfection take.

11 If even this exceeds your power
    from fruit of every act abstain
    and turning to my discipline
    perform your work but self restrain.

12 Wisdom is more than exercise,
    to meditate is more than wise,
    leaving fruits more than to meditate,
    leaving them brings peace immediate.

13 Be compassionate and friendly
    released from ego selfishness,
    patient, not hating any being,
    the same in pain and happiness.

14 The disciplined who stays content
    with thoughts and mind on me intent
    is self-controlled inflexibly,
    he loves me and is dear to me.

In six of the following
seven verses the devotee
is called dear to or loved
by God

15 By him the world is not disturbed
and by the world he's not perturbed,
from joy and fear and rashness free,
untroubled, he is dear to me.

16 Pure, capable and unconcerned,
unswayed by party anxiety,
with not a selfish enterprise
he loves me and is dear to me.

17 The one who neither loves nor loathes,
no good or evil things would see,
who never grieves and never craves
is full of love and dear to me.

18 Unmoved by honour or disgrace,
to friend and enemy the same,
detached from sorrow and from joy
in cold and heat he stays the same.

19 Reserved alike in blame and praise,
content that any lot may be,
with steady mind that homeless man
is full of love and dear to me.

20 Yes, those who hold this deathless nectar
of Right and concentrate on me
having faith as I declared it
are the devotees most dear to me.

SO ENDS
THE TWELFTH CHAPTER
AND ITS NAME IS
the Yoga of
Loving Devotion

13
Distinction of Field and Field-knower

The Blessed Lord said:

1 This body here is named the Field
and he who comprehends is called
by those who understand such things
the Knower of this very Field.

The body, and Nature in general, is the Field in which things grow and die, a place of constant activity

2 I am the Knower of the Field
in every Field and hold it so
that you must see this is true knowledge
the Knower and the Field to know.

The Field-knower is the Soul, detaching and knowing. God is the supreme knower of all fields

3 What the Field is, what its nature,
what its changes, whence these may be,
who he is and what his powers
in brief you will understand from me.

He, the Field-knower

4 Once in the various Vedic hymns
sages sang this in ways diverse,
well reasoned out and definite
and also in Brahmanic verse.

5 The Unmanifested and the mind,
the ego and the gross elements,
the eleven senses forming part,
and five objects for the play of sense.

Twenty-four categories: Nature as Unmanifest or primal matter and its evolutes: mind, ego, five gross elements, five organs of knowledge, five of action, and reason, and five objects of senses

6 With various changes, thus the Field
is here described in brevity:
in desire and hatred, joy and pain,
their joining, thought and constancy.

7   To lack conceit and not deceive,
    with patience, honour, harmlessness,
    to serve a teacher in purity
    with self-control and steadiness.

8   Detached from objects of the sense
    and understanding the worthlessness
    of birth and death, old age, disease,
    and pain, and leaving selfishness.

9   Detached, with no excessive love
    for sons and wife and home and all,
    in constant evenness of mind
    if loved or unloved things befall.

10 With never-swerving love to me
    and single-minded discipline,
    dwelling in the lonely places
    dissatisfied with crowds of men.

11 Seek wisdom that concerns the soul
    and see where knowing truth will lead;
    all else is only ignorance
    but this is wisdom, so 'tis said.

12 This is the thing to know, and knowing
    a man attains to deathlessness,
    'tis neither Being nor Non-being,
    the Highest Brahman, beginningless.

The supreme Person or
Spirit has hands and feet
on all sides and enfolds
all. Rig Veda 10, 90;
Shvetashvatara Upanishad
3, 16

13 It has hands and feet on every side,
    eyes, heads and mouths on all the sides,
    ears on all sides and in the world
    embracing all it still abides.

It has the semblance of
Qualities or Strands in
all senses

14 With Qualities like every sense
    and yet released from every sense,
    detached and free from Qualities
    it holds and feels the Qualities.

15 Within all beings yet outside
   while moving this is motionless,
   it stands far off and yet is near,
   not understood thro' its subtleness.

16 Both undivided in all beings
   yet seems divided this remains,
   it should be known as creating beings
   which both consumes and yet sustains.

17 This is also the Light of lights,
   Beyond the Darkness, this they call,
   knowledge, the known, the goal of knowledge,
   established in the heart of all.

18 So the Field and also knowledge
   and the object of knowledge I declare,
   my devotee who comprehends
   in my own mode of being will share.

19 Know that Nature and the Spirit
   had no beginning equally,
   know that Qualities and changes
   alone from Nature come to be.

Nature and Spirit are both eternal, but the Qualities come from Nature alone

20 In cause, effect and agency
   that Nature is declared the cause,
   of experiencing in joy and pain
   the Spirit is declared the cause.

21 For the Spirit lodged in Nature
   feels the Qualities from Nature come,
   but grasping Qualities will cause
   rebirth in a good or evil womb.

The Spirit experiences the Qualities of Nature but attachment to them brings rebirth

22 The Highest Spirit in this body
   is called the Highest Soul who moves
   and feels, and as the Mighty Lord
   and as Spectator he approves.

The Highest Spirit is God himself

23 Whosoever knows the Spirit
    and Nature with each Quality
    will never be reborn again
    in whatsoever state he be.

24 By meditation, in the soul
    some by themselves perceive the Soul,
    and some by Reason-discipline,
    others by Action-discipline.

25 There are some without this knowledge
    who hear from others, these revere
    and they cross over death as well
    intent upon the word they hear.

The Field and the Knower
are considered again as
the joining of matter and
spirit

26 In so far as any creature
    moving or motionless may become
    know that from union of the Field
    with the Field-knower this has sprung.

27 Whoever sees the Highest Lord
    dwelling alike in every being,
    not decaying when they perish,
    that man indeed is truly seeing.

The Highest Soul is in all
and when other souls
realize that they cannot
be hurt

28 And when he sees this very Lord
    abides the same throughout the whole,
    then he himself harms not the self
    but goes towards the highest goal.

29 He who understands that Nature
    does every act in every deed,
    that his own self acts not at all
    in any way, he sees indeed.

See 3, 27

30 When he perceives the varied state
    of beings that abide in One
    and out of which they radiate,
    then on to Brahman he has come.

31 This Highest Soul, unchangeable,
   tho' in the body this remains
   has no beginning, no Qualities,
   it never acts and gets no stains.

The Supreme Self has no
Qualities or attributes and
even when acting in the
world and in a body it is
not defiled by action

32 As ether present everywhere
   thro' its subtlety is undefiled,
   the Soul is present everywhere
   in bodies but is undefiled.

33 And just as all alone the sun
   lights up the world and everyone,
   so does the Owner of the Field
   illuminate the total Field.

34 Those who Field and Knower seeing
   as different, by wisdom's eye,
   released from Nature, cause of being,
   proceed towards the One most High.

SO ENDS
THE THIRTEENTH CHAPTER
AND ITS NAME IS
*the Yoga of
Distinction of
Field and Field-knower*

14
Distinction of the Three Qualities

The Blessed Lord said:

An account of creation as the primal union of God with Nature, here called Brahman

1 The highest wisdom I shall tell,
the wisdom that is best of all
and comprehending which all saints
gained full perfection passing hence.

2 Taking refuge in this wisdom
they get a state akin to mine,
never born at world creation,
unmoved at dissolution time.

3 For me Great Brahman is a womb
and I have placed the seed therein
out of which comes every being
taking from that its origin.

4 Whatever kind of form indeed
originates in any womb,
I am the Father giving seed
and that Great Brahman acts as womb.

A detailed study follows of the three Qualities or Strands of Nature

5 These three—Goodness, Passion, Darkness,
are Qualities that from Nature spring,
the embodied and unchanging soul
in the body they are fettering.

Goodness (*sattva*), purity or brightness, is the best Quality and yet it can bind the embodied soul

6 Among these Goodness, immaculate,
will healthily illuminate
yet bind the soul, attaching this
to wisdom or with bonds of bliss.

7 Then Passion which is full of lust
springs from attachment and from thirst,
and this will bind the embodied one
attaching it to actions done.

Passion (*rajas*), energy, or force

8 And Darkness, born of ignorance,
attaches men with heedlessness,
deluding all embodied souls
by means of sloth and sleepiness.

Darkness (*tamas*), or mass

9 Goodness attaches man to bliss,
Passion to action's influence,
Darkness by obscuring wisdom
attaches him to negligence.

10 Goodness will grow if it prevail
over Passion and Dark as well,
Darkness by ruling Passion and Good,
Passion by ruling Dark and Good.

11 But when the light of wisdom shines
at every one of the body's gates
in this event you recognize
that Goodness fully dominates.

See 5, 13

12 When Passion comes to dominate
these are conditions that arise—
activity, disquiet and greed,
ambition, craving enterprise.

13 When Darkness comes to dominate
a lack of light and laziness
are the conditions that appear
with deluded mind and heedlessness.

14 If the embodied soul arrives
at dissolution when Goodness reigns
then to the spotless worlds of men
who know the Highest he attains.

Dying when dominated by
Passion and reborn among
those attached to action

15 But a man dissolved in Passion
is born among the action-bound,
and a man dissolved in Darkness
among deluded wombs is found.

16 Men say about an act well done
and spotless this is Goodness' fruit,
the fruit of Passion comes as pain
and ignorance is Darkness' fruit.

17 Wisdom is derived from Goodness
but out of Passion rises greed,
ignorance derives from Darkness
with delusion and a lack of heed.

18 The men of Goodness rise on high,
the men of Passion in the middle go,
but held in the basest Quality
the men of Darkness go below.

See 3, 28

19 When the observing soul perceives
no agent but the Qualities
he finds my mode of being and knows
One higher than the Qualities.

20 Transcending these three Qualities
of the body's life, the soul is free
from birth and age, from death and grief,
achieving immortality.

Arjuna said:

See 2, 54

21 What sort of signs will mark him out
when man transcends these Qualities?
just how should he behave and how
transcend all these three Qualities?

The Blessed Lord said:

22 He neither seeks illumination,
delusion nor activities,
he does not loathe them when they rise
nor hanker for them when they cease.

23 He sits as one indifferent
whom the Qualities have not perturbed,
he thinks 'the Qualities are at work',
remaining firm and undisturbed.

See 9, 9

See 3, 28 and 5, 9

24 Self-assured in pain and pleasure,
with clods and stones and gold the same,
to whom unloved and loved are equal,
the wise holds equal praise and blame.

See 6, 8

25 Alike in honour and disgrace
to allies and to enemies,
renouncing every enterprise
this man transcends the Qualities.

26 One who transcends these Qualities,
intent on me and never swerves,
is fitted for becoming Brahman
if in discipline of love he serves.

See 5, 24

27 I am the Ground of Brahman still
immortal and unchangeable,
of everlasting righteousness
and of invariable bliss.

God the foundation of
Brahman, see 10, 12 and
15, 18

SO ENDS
THE FOURTEENTH CHAPTER
AND ITS NAME IS
The Yoga of
Distinction of
the Three Qualities

15
The Supreme Spirit

The Blessed Lord said:

The Pipal or Bo-tree is a symbol of the world and the round of birth and rebirth. Its root is above, its branches below, this eternal fig-tree; Katha Upanishad 6, 1

Long metre

1 The changeless Fig-tree, men say so,
has roots that rise and branches low,
its very leaves are Vedic hymns,
who know this all the Veda know.

2 Its branches issue up and down, their shoots
sense-objects fed by Qualities, its roots
extend below and in the human world
result in all activity's pursuits.

Cut down the tree of reincarnation and take refuge in the Primal Spirit from whose highest home there is no return to earth

3 Yet thus no form of it we comprehend,
not its beginning, basis, or its end;
this Fig-tree then with firmly growing roots
detachment's mighty axe must cut and rend.

4 Then one should seek the place to which
    men go
and having found return no more below:
'to that Primeval Spirit I resort
from whom creative acts came long ago.'

5 Deluded not nor proud, detached they gain
their freedom from the Pairs of joy and pain,
desire suppressed, firm as concerns the soul,
the undeceived that changeless state attain.

6 That state is not illuminated
by either sun or moon or fire,
men go there and do not return,
that is my home and none is higher.

7 A part of me in the world of life,
eternal, becomes a living soul,
attracting to itself a mind
and sense which Nature makes a whole.

8 When this lord acquires a body
and also when he goes therefrom
he takes these with him while he moves
as wind blows scents away from home.

The lord is here the
individual soul as
sovereign of the body

9 Hearing and sight, and touch and taste
he operates in confidence,
along with reasoning and smell
attending to the things of sense.

10 He feels by means of Qualities,
he leaves the body or stays thereby,
deluded men perceive him not
but they see him who have wisdom's eye.

11 The disciplined strive earnestly
and see him fixed within the soul,
but fools however much they strive
see him not thro' their imperfect soul.

12 There is a splendour in the sun
that all the world illuminates,
a splendour in the fire and moon
and from my being all radiates.

13 And penetrating into earth
all beings by power I maintain,
also becoming dewy juice
all healing simples I sustain.

14 Then I become digestive power
in forms of everything with breath
and food of all kinds I devour
conjoined with in and outward breath.

Long metre

15 I dwell within the hearts of all and so
   from me come memory, wisdom and their

Flow, loss, removal of
doubt

      flow,
   thro' all the Vedas I alone am known,
   Vedanta's author, I the Veda know.

The selves in Nature and
the Brahman without
qualities, see 8, 3-4

16 In this world there are two spirits,
   the perishable and the Imperishable,
   the perishable is moving beings,
   the Imperishable is immutable.

17 There is yet a Higher Spirit,
   the One they call the Highest Soul,
   the unchanging Lord who enters in
   the three worlds and supports them all.

18 In the world and in the Vedas
   since I transcend the perishable,
   I am called the Highest Spirit
   and higher than the Imperishable.

19 The man who recognizes me
   as Highest Spirit knows everything
   and undeluded comes to me
   with all his love and all his being.

20 So you've heard me at last reveal
   the most mysterious words of all
   and enlightened here with wisdom true
   you have finished all that you must do.

SO ENDS
THE FIFTEENTH CHAPTER
AND ITS NAME IS
the Yoga of the Supreme Spirit

16
Distinction of Divine and Demonic States

The Blessed Lord said:

1 These are the attributes of one
who is born to the Divine Estate—
ardour, patience, strength and cleanness,
without conceit and lacking hate.

2 A fearless man and pure in heart
with disciplined wisdom and steadfastness,
generous restraint and sacrifice,
study and ascetic uprightness.

3 Renunciation, without lies or wrath,
serenity, harmlessness and truth,
modesty, without greed or fickleness,
kindness to beings and gentleness.

4 The attributes of one whose fate
is birth in the Demonic State
are hypocrisy, wrath and insolence,
conceit and pride and ignorance.

5 The Demonic Destiny enslaves,
the Divine Condition sets you free,
but you have never cause to grieve
as born to Godly Destiny.

6 Two groups of beings in the world
are the divine and those demoniac,
the divine I have explained at length
now hear me on the demoniac.

G

7 Demonic people never learn
   creative work and then return,
   one finds in them no purity,
   no truth or sound morality.

Materialists say there is
no Creator but desire is
the cause of all

8 They say the world displays no truth,
   no God and no religious laws,
   it only functions by desire
   not as result of ordered cause.

9 Holding fast to this opinion
   lost souls of weak intelligence
   are enemies who destroy the world
   by cruel deeds and violence.

10 Mad with hypocrisy and pride
   they clutch unsatisfied desire,
   deluded by untrue ideas
   to dirty business men aspire.

11 Devoted to such boundless cares
   that last till death, their highest goal
   is satisfying appetites
   being convinced that these are all.

12 Tied by a hundred bonds of hope,
   by anger and desire obsessed,
   obtaining wealth by wrongful means
   in order to enjoy their lust.

The rich fool speaks

13 'Behold the riches I have gained
   and pleasures next to be obtained,
   I own this wealth and also mine
   are riches of another time.

14 'There is an enemy I slew
   and later I'll kill others too,
   I am the master, joys belong
   to me, successful, happy, strong.

15 'I am wealthy, of noble line
   and none can be compared with mine.
   I shall give alms, rejoice, and pray'—
   Confused by ignorance they say.

16 Entangled in delusion's net
   and fooled by many a fancied spell,
   seeking enjoyment of desires
   they tumble to a filthy hell.

17 In arrogance and self-conceit,
   maddened by pride and avarice,
   in name alone and not by rule
   such hypocrites make sacrifice.

18 These envious men in egotism,
   in force and wrath, desire and pride,
   detest me whether in their own
   or others' bodies I abide.   See 17, 6

19 Within this transmigrating place
   I ever cast these wicked men,
   the cruel, hateful and the base
   into demonic wombs again.   For the opposite see 12, 7

20 Born again to demonic wombs
   and not attaining me at all,
   deluded still from birth to birth
   down to the lowest way they fall.

21 Here is the triple door of hell—
   in Anger and Desire and Greed,
   and as destructive of the soul
   from all these three one must be freed.

22 But whenever man can practise
   the work that benefits his soul,
   freed from these three doors of Darkness
   he goes towards the highest goal.

23 One who neglects the law's command
   in living by desire and whim,
   perfection now and later bliss
   and the highest goal are not for him.

24 Therefore the law must be your guide
   and what to do or not decide,
   perceiving that the law's behest
   will make your action here the best.

SO ENDS
THE SIXTEENTH CHAPTER
AND ITS NAME IS
the Yoga of Distinction
of Divine and Demonic States

17
Distinction of Three Kinds of Faith

Arjuna said:

1 Some men may worship full of faith
and yet neglect the law's command—
is it in Goodness or in Passion
or else in Darkness these may stand?

The three Qualities of
Nature in every man
determine the kind of
faith and action, see 6, 37

The Blessed Lord said:

2 Embodied souls may have three kinds
of faith that from their being appear,
marked by Goodness or by Passion
or Darkness, and of each you'll hear.

Three kinds of Faith

3 Surely the faith of every man
with his own nature must agree,
since man is here composed of faith
and as his faith is so is he.

4 Good men to gods pay sacrifice,
Passionate men serve the giants and sprites,
but men of Darkness worship ghosts
and reverence departed hosts.

5 The men who keep austerity
beyond what any laws require,
with egotism, hypocrisy,
with passion, violence, desire,

6 Such fools are starving in their body
not just their elemental frame
but starve me also in their body—
so know demoniac their aim.

See 16, 18

7 The food that every man enjoys
   has three distinct varieties,
   and similar distinctiveness
   is in worship, alms and austerities.

Three kinds of Food

8 The Foods that men of Goodness like
   are those that fuller life impart,
   give courage, strength, and health and joy,
   rich, tasty, firm and warm the heart.

9 A cause of sorrow, pain and sickness
   is Food that Passion's men devour,
   the sharp and stringent burning things,
   the pungent, salty, hot and sour.

10 The Food a man of Darkness loves
   is stale and tasteless or is made
   unfitted for a sacrifice,
   with what is rotten, stale, decayed.

Three kinds of Worship
or Sacrifice

11 Worship that derives from Goodness
   is mind-controlled and keeps the law,
   not seeking for rewards because
   this work is duty, nothing more.

12 Worship that derives from Passion
   is that which certain people pay
   for the sake of getting the rewards
   with hypocritical display.

13 Worship that derives from Darkness,
   no fees will give or texts recite,
   as utterly devoid of faith,
   no alms are paid, no proper rite.

Austerity or ascetic
practice in Body, Speech,
and Mind

14 This is Austerity of Body
   in pureness, homage, uprightness,
   to teachers, priests and gods and sages
   in chastity and harmlessness.

15 This is Austerity of Speech
   in words that never cause unease,
   with study of the sacred texts,
   truthful and kind and keen to please.

16 This is Austerity of Mind
   with tranquil thought, benignity,
   in silence and in self-restraint
   and in one's being purity.

17 Austerity produced by Goodness   Three kinds of Austerity
   is manifested thus threefold
   by men who have the highest faith
   without rewards and self-controlled.

18 Austerity produced by Passion
   for honour, welcome, reverence,
   is done in sheer hypocrisy
   is fickle and lacks permanence.

19 Austerity produced by Darkness
   comes from deluded theory
   and aims at torturing oneself
   or another man's calamity.

20 The Gift that is derived from Goodness   Three kinds of Gifts or
   aspires for no returning grace,   Alms
   but gives because it must be done
   to a worthy man and time and place.

21 But that Gift derives from Passion
   which seeks returning grace from some,
   and is either given grudgingly
   or aiming at rewards to come.

22 And this Gift is made by Darkness
   to an unworthy recipient
   at any wrongful place or time,
   without respect and shows contempt.

OM, the sacred syllable
begins and ends ritual
utterances, see 7, 8
TAT, that, the impersonal
divine
SAT, reality, as goodness

23 OM, TAT, SAT—has been recorded
to make the Brahman sign threefold
by the priests and in the Vedas
were sacrifices fixed of old.

24 Therefore after pronouncing OM
with worship, gifts and austerity
the priestly students do their work
as verses say that such must be.

25 With THAT, and seeking no rewards,
their gifts of all varieties,
acts of sacrifice and penance,
are done by men who seek release.

SAT, it is, reality

26 In meaning REAL and meaning GOOD
IT IS is properly employed,
and also of commended work
IT IS is worthily enjoyed.

27 In worship, alms and austerities
is steadfastness considered REAL
and with such purposes in mind
action is also known as REAL.

28 But what is offered lacking faith,
in alms or penance, rite or text,
can only be declared UNREAL
with naught in this world, naught the next.

SO ENDS
THE SEVENTEENTH CHAPTER
AND ITS NAME IS
*the Yoga of
Distinction of
Three Kinds of Faith*

18
Renunciation and Salvation

Arjuna said:

1 Finally I would know the truth
as it concerns Abandonment
and about Renunciation
where each of them is different.

The Blessed Lord said:

2 Renouncing actions of desire
is what Renunciation meant,
abandoning rewards of acts
the wise have called Abandonment.

3 Some wise men say every action
must all be given up as ill,
others say that acts of worship,
penance and alms you must fulfil.

4 Listen to my own decision
in this business of Abandonment
for in such a manner is declared
a threefold self-abandonment.

5 You must do and not abandon
austerity, alms and sacrifice,
for sacrifice, alms and austerity
are acts that purify the wise.

6 However, these actions must be done
always abandoning reward
and attachment, for this judgement
is my supreme and final word.

The difference between
renunciation of all actions
and abandonment of
rewards, considered in
Chapter 5, is raised again
and the following verses
discuss behaviour
according to the three
Qualities

Three kinds of
Abandonment or
Surrender

7 Abandonment belongs to Darkness
when abandoning an act required
and doing this improperly
for by delusion 'tis inspired.

8 Abandonment belongs to Passion
and will not realize success
if one abandons it for trouble
and fear of bodily distress.

9 Abandonment belongs to Goodness
when work required is well begun,
detached, abandoning rewards,
because it simply must be done.

10 Full of Goodness, a surrendered man
will never hate unpleasant work,
and the wise who has his doubts destroyed
will neither cling to pleasant work.

11 While in the body no one can
without remainder abandon work
but he who abandons fruits of work
is called a self-surrendered man.

Fruits of varied actions in
three levels of rebirth

12 Undesired, desired and mingled—
are threefold fruits of works for men
after death for the unsurrendered
but never for renouncing men.

Five causes or factors
involved in action

13 In the Reason-method system
five major factors are declared
and if you learn from me all acts
will be effectively prepared.

The basis is the body, the
instruments are the senses,
Fate comes from the
divine

14 The material basis, and the agent,
and instruments of many a kind,
with great variety of motions,
and Fate the fifth and last you find.

15 Whatever work one undertakes
these five factors to that belong,
in the body, in the mind, and speech,
no matter whether right or wrong.

16 That being so, the man who thinks
the agent is his self alone
because his judgement is untrained
does not see truly, foolish one.

Nature, not the self, is
the agent, see 3, 27

17 But one who is not an egotist,
whose mind is nowhere stained by ill,
even tho' he slays these people
is not bound by that and does not kill.

See 2, 19

18 Knowledge, object and the knower
compose the threefold cause of work,
instrument and act and agent
compose the threefold sum of work.

19 Knowledge, action and the agent
in the theory of the Qualities
differ in Quality and are three in kind
so listen to the way of these.

The Qualities in
Knowledge, Action, Agent,
Mind, Constancy, and
Happiness in the following
verses

20 Be sure that Knowledge comes from
Goodness
where men a changeless state are seeing,
undivided yet divided,
the same in every kind of being.

Three kinds of Knowledge

21 But the Knowledge comes from Passion
which in all types of beings finds
distinction and difference in modes
of varied sorts and many kinds.

22 And the Knowledge comes from Darkness
which holds to one effect as all,
not bothered with causality
but is narrow and ignores the Real.

Three kinds of Action
(*karma*)

23 Action is derived from Goodness
   when done without desire or hate,
   if obligatory and detached
   by those who no rewards await.

24 Action is derived from Passion
   which heavy energy expends
   on gratifying one's own pleasures
   and simply for his selfish ends.

25 Action is derived from Darkness
   in disregarding consequence
   with loss or harm to self and others
   because of one's deluded sense.

Three kinds of Agent

26 Next, the Agent comes from Goodness
   with energy and steadfastness,
   detached and free from egotism,
   the same in failure or success.

27 That Agent is derived from Passion
   who joys and grieves, and would procure
   rewards of work, is passionate,
   injurious, covetous, impure.

28 And that Agent comes from Darkness,
   the undisciplined and proud and low,
   dishonest, lazy and a cheat,
   depressed and dilatory and slow.

29 Distinguish Mind and Constancy
   as threefold by their Qualities,
   listen as I show them fully
   in their several varieties.

Three kinds of Mind

30 First that Mind belongs to Goodness
   where bondage and release are known,
   cessation, work and fear and calm,
   with things to do and not be done.

31 Then that Mind belongs to Passion
   which misconceives what things belong,
   in acting or in doing nothing,
   to what is right or what is wrong.

32 And that Mind belongs to Darkness
   which understands the wrong as right,
   and all the opposite to truth
   because that Dark obscures the light.

33 Constancy derives from Goodness   Three kinds of Constancy
   when one restrains activities   or Firmness
   of mind and breath and every sense
   in constant steadfast exercise.

34 Constancy derives from Passion
   when constantly a man holds tight,
   attached and seeking for rewards,
   in wealth or in desire or right.   See 7, 16

35 Constancy derives from Darkness
   wherein a fool puts not aside
   his sorrow, cowardice or sleep
   or his despondency or pride.

36 And last the threefold Happiness
   which I'll expound if you attend,
   that which one enjoys thro' practice
   and making sorrow come to end.

37 First the Happiness of Goodness   Three kinds of Happiness
   when mind and soul's serenity
   at the first appears like poison
   but nectar in maturity.

38 Then the Happiness of Passion
   from joining objects to each sense   Coming from the union of
   at the first appears like nectar   senses with their objects
   but poison in the consequence.

39 And the Happiness of Darkness
is that which leads the soul astray,
derived from careless sloth and sleep,
both first and at the end, they say.

40 For there is nothing on the earth
and in heaven no divinities

All beings are bound by
the Strands of Nature

no being free from that which comes
from these three Natural Qualities.

The special duties of each
of the four classes of
society

41 For priests and warriors, and then
for artisans and serfs, all these
have activities distributed
by inborn proper Qualities.

42 For Priests the natural work is faith,
control and patience, quietness,
in theory as in practised wisdom,
with austerity and uprightness.

43 A Warrior's natural work is skill
with lordly generosity,
in never fleeing from the fight
but courage, firmness, majesty.

44 For Artisans 'tis natural work
to trade and herd and till the soil,
and Servants have their natural work
in service that consists of toil.

Special work, one's own
proper action

45 Rejoicing in his special work
a man attains perfectedness,
hear how he may achieve success
rejoicing in his special work.

46 For a man attains perfection
with his own action worshipping

The One by whom the
universe was spun and
from whom comes activity

the One who fills this universe,
source of activity of being.

47 Much better do one's duty ill
   than do another's duty well,   Partly the same as 3, 35
   doing the duty that pertains
   to one's own state incurs no stains.

48 And even tho' it has its faults
   do not abandon your proper work,
   for every enterprise by faults
   is clouded as a fire by smoke.

49 With mind detached from any object,
   self-conquered and from longings free,
   man finds by renunciation
   the perfect inactivity.   Perfection of
                              actionlessness

50 Having first achieved perfection
   how Brahman also you may gain
   as the highest goal of wisdom
   listen as briefly I explain.

51 Restraining self with constancy,
   cleansed by an integrated mind,
   abandon loathing and desire,
   leave sound and sensual things behind.

52 With body, speech and thought controlled
   in solitude eat less and less,   See 6, 10
   always practise meditation
   and cultivate desirelessness.

53 Fitted for becoming Brahman   See 5, 24
   beyond aggression, pride and greed,
   unselfish, calm, from egotism
   desire and anger you are freed.

54 Becoming Brahman, calm in soul,
   not coveting or disagreeing,
   he wins the highest love to me   The highest love (*bhakti*)
   and is the same to every being.   for God after becoming
                                       Brahman's fixed still state

55 By love he comes to recognize
my greatness, who I really am
and enters into me at once
by knowing me as I really am.

56 Altho' by putting trust in me
one may all actions operate
'tis by my grace that he achieves
the eternal and unchanging state.

57 Make me your goal and by your thought
be all your works to me resigned,
devoted to me constantly
resort to discipline of mind.

Turning from general
teaching to special needs

58 Thinking of me, by my own grace
all difficulties shall be crossed,
but if because of egotism
you will not listen you are lost.

59 If you cling to your egotism
your resolution will be vain

See 2, 9

imagining 'I will not fight'
for your Nature will to this constrain.

60 Held fast by your natural action
whatever you try not to do
in the blindness of delusion
against your will perforce you'll do.

God dwells in all beings
and makes them move like
puppets in a play, the
machine is the universe

61 In the heart of every being
the Lord abides and every being
he causes by his power to spin
around as fixed in his machine.

See verse 66

62 Go to him alone for refuge
with all your being, by his grace
you will attain the highest peace
and his eternal resting place.

63 This wisdom as explained by me
   is mystery of mystery
   and when you've fully pondered it
   behave as you consider fit.

64 The greatest mystery of all
   my highest word be understood—
   you are so greatly loved by me
   that I shall tell your real good.

The return of divine love
for human loving devotion

65 Show love to me, bear me in mind,
   offer me worship and revere,
   I promise you will come to me
   because you are to me so dear.

See 12, 14–20

66 Abandoning all things of law
   to me alone you must repair,
   from every evil evermore
   I shall release you, have no care.

The favourite final verse
held to be the climax and
summary of the Gita

67 But you must never speak of this
   to whosoever lives without
   austerity or envies me,
   is disobedient or undevout.

68 He who tells this highest secret
   to my own devotees will show
   the highest reverent love to me
   and without a doubt to me shall go.

69 Nobody else of human kind
   does anything to me more dear
   nor shall there ever be on earth
   another one to me more dear.

70 Whosoever comes to study
   our dialogue concerning right,
   with a sacrifice of wisdom,
   he worships me to my delight.

The discussion of duty or
this sacred dialogue

H

71 And one who simply hears with faith
    and murmurs not at this, proceeds
    to find release and the happy worlds
    where dwell the men of virtuous deeds.

72 Have you attended to these words
    with thoughts in concentration held?
    and since it came from ignorance
    is your confusion now dispelled?

The confusion about right
action and the true nature
of the soul with which the
Gita began

Arjuna said:

73 Yes, my confusion is destroyed
    attending to the truth I heard
    and thro' your grace with doubts dispersed
    I stand and shall obey your word.

The charioteer concludes
with the final setting for
the blind king, see 1, 1–2

Samjaya said:

74 Thus I heard from Vasudeva
    and Arjuna, the Mighty Soul,
    I listened to their dialogue
    and it was thrilling, wonderful.

Vyasa, author of the Gita,
gave Samjaya power to
see and hear all

75 For I heard by grace of Vyasa
    of Krishna's highest mystery,
    Yoga from the Lord of Yoga
    himself explaining personally.

76 As I remember and recall
    the discourse wondrous, most sublime
    which Krishna held with Arjuna
    I thrill with pleasure every time.

77 And more and more I thrill with joy
    as I remember and recall
    the bewildering astonishment

The form of Vishnu in
the vision, Chapter 11

    of Vishnu's most wondrous form of all.

78 Where Krishna, Yoga-Lord, may be,
   wherever Arjuna lifts his bow,
   there fortune, welfare, victory
   and statecraft stand—for this I know.

SO ENDS
THE EIGHTEENTH CHAPTER
AND ITS NAME IS
*the Yoga of
Renunciation and Salvation*

Appendix

Appendix

Setting and Purpose

The Maha-bharata, the Great Bharata or India epic, is a vast compilation of national legend, religious mythology, and theological and philosophical teaching. Its central theme is the struggle for sovereignty between the Kurus and their cousins the Pandus. The eldest of the five Pandu brothers, Yudhi-shthira, had been nominated king by the blind Kuru king, Dhrita-rashtra; but through the jealousy of the latter's son, Dur-yodhana, and having lost all his belongings in gambling, Yudhi-shthira and his brothers went into exile in the forest. Twelve years later the Pandu princes with their common wife Draupadi, returned to fight the Kurus for their kingdom. After many battles the Pandus won, losing their children and friends. Having reigned for a time, Yudhi-shthira abdicated and retired with his brothers to the Himalayas where finally all died.

In the epic the god Krishna appears to help the Pandus and he acts as charioteer to the third brother, Arjuna. Krishna, 'dark', is little known in earlier Indian verse but he now receives many titles: Bhagavat, Lord; Govinda, cow-keeper; Vasudeva, and so on. Krishna was perhaps an old tribal hero and god who came to be identified with Vishnu, a god of the Veda hymns; this identification is not very clear in the Gita, except in the vision of chapter 11. Later Krishna was called Avatara, or Avatar, a 'down-coming' or 'embodiment' of God. This word does not occur in the Gita, but in 4, 7 it is clearly stated that 'I send myself to birth' whenever Right is languishing. Krishna is further identified in the Gita with the Supreme Brahman, and is called Primal God, Highest Abode, and Eternal Spirit. He is set forth as the ultimate God, who is yet personally manifested in the world when need arises. Though God may be known and served in various ways, through knowledge, works or renunciation, yet loving devotion (*bhakti*) is the highest and best way to him, for all kinds of people (12, 5–6).

The Bhagavad Gita, the Song of the Lord (Krishna), comes in the sixth book of the Maha-bharata. The author of the epic, Vyasa, offered to open blind Dhrita-rashtra's eyes to view the impending battle; but he could not bear the sight and so his charioteer, Samjaya, received the power of knowing all the actions and hearing the discussions that took place between Krishna and Arjuna.

Summary

The first word of the Gita sets the tone, 'the Field of Right', justice or duty (*Dharma-kshetre*), giving the concern of the poem with Arjuna's duty and universal right. Kuru and Pandu armies face each other and the chief heroes are named, suggesting a new development in the epic story. The god Krishna appears as Arjuna's charioteer, gives him a view of the armies, and despair falls on Arjuna since men and families will be destroyed in the battle and *dharma* will be broken. Arjuna decides not to fight and sits down in bewilderment.

Chapter 2 opens with a repetition of objections to fighting and then the Gita, the Lord's Song proper, begins at verse 11 with Krishna's teachings. His first theme is that the soul or embodied self is indestructible, it cannot kill or be killed. This implies belief in reincarnation, for what dies must be reborn. Further, Arjuna must perform his princely duty and not be a coward. Verse 39 turns to Yoga, which with many subtle variations is developed throughout the poem. Reason-method (Samkhya) taught the indestructibility of the soul, but Discipline-method (Yoga) gives guidance for action. Other ways are rejected, and action is demanded but with renunciation of rewards. The man of steady wisdom is described and his attainment of the Calm of eternity.

Chapter 3 seeks to reconcile the discipline of mind with the necessity for action, showing that all must act, but wise men renounce results. Action is done by the gods, by the imperishable

Brahman, by noble men, and by God himself (22–24) who has no need to act but does so to sustain the world. The self or soul is not involved in action, that comes from the Qualities or constituents of Nature, and so man must resign his actions to God and find release. Yet men do evil against their will, urged by passion, and the wise must rise above this.

Chapter 4 declares that this doctrine is eternal and that the deity had been born into the world age after age to maintain right. Knowledge of this brings release from transmigration. Actions must be performed, but in detachment. Various sacrifices are identified with works, but wisdom is best of all.

Chapter 5 shows that both renunciation and disciplined action are good, but the wise man is above contamination, for he is fully integrated and gives his actions to God. His soul is fixed in the Calm of Brahman, becoming immortal but at the last verse finding refuge in the Great Lord of all the worlds.

Chapter 6 shows that the lower self must be conquered by the higher Self. A short description is given of the Yoga of meditation, which brings absorption into God. Discipline brings calm and the vision of God in everything. The way is hard because of the fickleness of the mind, so that practice is needed and perseverance, but those who get on the right road can continue their progress in another life.

The great commentator Ramanuja said that the first six chapters of the Gita are concerned with knowledge of the soul and the next six with knowledge of God, psychology and theology. Some theology has already appeared, but chapter 7 proceeds to speak of the nature of God in the world and in the soul, in phenomena and in human qualities. Men who seek God in love are loved by him, and in whatever way men worship this has been divinely ordained, although the visible embodiment of the deity is not recognized by all yet those who do know it are liberated.

Chapter 8 speaks of divine manifestations and demands that man should fix his thoughts on God as the Highest Spirit and the Imperishable. The worlds emerge in cycles from unmanifested and manifested Nature, but beyond that there is the higher Unmanifest, the Supreme Spirit or Person, to whom the truly disciplined attain.

Chapter 9 develops the teaching of God pervading all things but not limited by them. All beings come from him though not all recognize him. He is indeed the ritual act and worship, the sacred formula, the father and mother of the universe. He cherishes the simplest offering (26), and all classes and both sexes can reach the highest goal (32), by love and devotion.

Chapter 10 shows the presence of the deity throughout the world. Gods and sages do not know his origin, because he is their origin, and all virtues like all creatures come from him. Arjuna bursts out in praise of the Primal Deity and seeks to understand his manifold powers so that he may meditate on God. Krishna lists his pervading powers, as the chief of all classes of beings, in man, in the gods, in nature, in all states and beings, yet this is only a fragment of his own being which remains unchanged and undiminished.

After these statements of divine immanence the way is clear for the divine transcendence, given in chapter 11 in heightened metre, in the most terrifying but fascinating picture of divinity in religious literature. Arjuna receives a divine eye to see the transcendental body of God, and his hair stands on end. The deity appears with countless eyes, mouths, arms, and bellies; all the gods are in his body which is hailed as the great God Vishnu. Into his great mouths all gods and saints enter, and all the heroes on the battlefield. This is Time or Doom, the end of a world-cycle, receiving all beings again into itself, and Arjuna is only the agent of the doom already fixed. Arjuna hails the All-God, the only true Deity, and then remembers that he has been over-familiar with the embodied Krishna and begs forgiveness. Krishna shows grace, takes back his human form, and comforts his friend. This vision is not given to gods, or gained by religious rituals, but only won by undivided love.

Chapter 12 is at a lower level but completes the picture of the worship of God. Those who seek an abstract divinity by the way of knowledge may attain to it, but the way is hard, whereas the Yoga of loving devotion is easy and God saves his loving servants from the sea of transmigration. The last seven verses repeat six times that God loves man.

The last six chapters of the Gita are more pedestrian, though there are flashes of feeling and the heights are climbed again at the end. Chapter 13 describes the body as a field of activity, the soul as the knower, and God as the supreme knower. The elements of the body and a list of virtues are given. The object of knowledge is the abstract Brahman but this is ruled by God and the supreme Lord abides in all beings.

Chapter 14 describes creation from the union of God with Brahman or Nature, and proceeds to study the three Qualities of Nature: Goodness, Passion, and Darkness, which occupy much of these later chapters. The soul must transcend these Qualities, detached from all, serving with love that God who is the foundation of Brahman and the basis of eternal right.

Chapter 15 describes the sacred Fig-tree as a symbol of the round of transmigration which must be cut down so that one may attain the highest home of the divinity. Parts of God come into the world to animate all things and are seen by the wise. Beyond the perishable and the imperishable is the supreme deity who should be known and loved.

Chapter 16 lists virtues and vices, and proceeds to describe the atheist and the rich fool. Such men do not get free from transmigration and so the wise should seek freedom from desire, anger and greed.

Chapter 17 distinguishes types of faith and criticizes exaggerated asceticism. The three Qualities of Nature operate in food, sacrifice, asceticism, and almsgiving. Sacred words represent goodness, truth, and reality.

Chapter 18 returns to the question of the abandonment of action or renunciation of rewards. Description continues of the three Qualities in different kinds of work, these are indicated again in the

four orders of society (from 41). From verse 50 the poem rises
again to the heights, speaking of perfection, Brahman, and union
with God. Love to God is the key to knowledge of his reality, and
to him man should go for refuge and find salvation by his grace.
The highest secret is that the lover of God is greatly loved by God
and he will save his follower from all evils. The closing verses
declare that Arjuna's doubts are resolved, he will obey the divine
instruction and do his duty. The memory of the divine-human
dialogue, and especially of the transcendental vision of the form of
God, brings joy and success.

Metre and Style

The Maha-bharata is a huge poem of 100,000 verses. In the sixth
book comes the Bhagavad Gita, relatively short, 700 verses in
18 chapters. The Gita is mostly composed in a metre (*anu-shtubh*
or *shloka*) of eight syllables to the line and four lines to a verse.
Occasionally it changes to a longer metre (*tri-shtubh*) of eleven
syllables to the line. The longer verses sometimes give repetition
but often they mark passages of high poetic or religious feeling,
as in the Vision in chapter 11, where thirty-six stanzas are in *tri-
shtubh*, or the opening verses on the Fig Tree in chapter 15. The
speeches in the dialogue are introduced with words, such as
'Arjuna said', which are not part of the verse but are prose
connecting the verse passages.

Every translation of the Gita is a rendering from Sanskrit verse
into some literary style of another language, and change of form is
bound to occur. Rhyme is not used in the Gita, apart from some
repetitions as in 1, 8, but there is a rhythm that is fixed by the
length or shortness of the syllables. Obviously this cannot be
reproduced in translation into the words of another language, and
English does not lend itself to a complicated system of long and
short vowels. But English is rich in poetic forms, and at least two
translators have made versions of the Gita largely in the ten-
syllable iambic verse, as used by Shakespeare. K. T. Telang in 1874
began chapter 1 like this:

What did my party and the Pandavs do
Oh Sanjaya when upon the Holy Field
Of Kurukshetra, longing for the fight
They met together?
                Seeing then the host
Of Pandu's sons, drawn up in battle array
The Prince Duryodhan to his teacher went . . .

Another poetical rendering was made by Sir Edwin Arnold in 1885, called *The Song Celestial*, beginning thus:

Ranged thus for battle on the sacred plain—
On Kurukshetra—say, Sanjaya, say
What wrought my people, and the Pandavas?

When he beheld the host of Pandavas
Raja Duryodhana to Drona drew,
And spake these words . . .

In 1911 C. G. Caleb produced an unrhymed translation in iambic metre but with an eight-syllable line:

On Kuru-field, the field of Right,
    Where Pandu's children and my sons
Resolved on war stand face to face
    Tell me, O Sanjay, how they fare.

The king Duryodhan when he saw
    The marshalled hosts of Pandu's sons,
Approached his old preceptor then,
    And unto him these words addressed . . .

These poetical attempts may be compared with the almost literal prose translation made by Franklin Edgerton, but set out in lines like verse, and published in 1944.

In the Field of Right, the Kuru-field,
    Assembled ready to fight,
My men and the sons of Pandu as well,
    What did they do, Samjaya?

> Seeing however the host of the sons of Pandu
>   Arrayed, Duryodhana then
> Approached the Teacher (Drona)
> And spoke a word, the prince . . .

To attempt some representation of the form as well as the contents of the Gita is clearly hazardous. To use eight syllables to the line, as in the Anushtubh, is fairly easy, but to attempt some correspondence to vowel lengths is much more difficult if not impossible. But in this metre the second and fourth lines always end in a double iambus (∪—∪ ×), and I have used English forms of an iambic metre to end the second and fourth lines of each verse of my rendering, and reinforced them with rhyme which English has traditionally used instead of vowel length. The rhymes thus given are usually between the second and fourth lines, but sometimes rhymes have been used in other lines as well. The first and third lines here have also usually been rendered in iambic form (∪—), but I have employed a trochaic metre (—∪) where it seemed to be suitable.

The elevated Trishtubh eleven-syllable verse is more difficult, and after some experiments it was decided not to attempt an approximation but to go frankly for the common English ten-syllable line, and try to heighten the effect with three rhymes to each verse. This involved adding a word occasionally, but it was always kept within the sense, or lines were inverted but with the same restriction.

The author of the Gita used many names and titles of Krishna and Arjuna, such as Keshava, Janardana, Partha, Paramtapa, and so on. These helped out the metre in Sanskrit but in translation they are a burden and their omission both gives extra play and removes the verse from particular to universal interest.

This book is the result of more than twelve years' work during which time every verse, almost every word, has been revised scores of times. It aims at being modern and direct, without poetic fancies, archaic coyness or theological distortion. The standard Sanskrit text has been followed and the best English translations were studied, especially the prose versions of W. D. P. Hill, F. Edgerton, and R. C. Zaehner. This work is not meant as a new critical translation, and interesting questions of textual and doctrinal criticism have been left aside. The purpose is to provide a popular yet accurate rendering, which will help readers to memorize important verses and understand the teachings of the Bhagavad Gita.

Pronunciation

Little has been done to mark pronunciation, except in the simplest way, and dots and accents that might confuse the general reader have been omitted.

Sanskrit s and ś have both been rendered as 'sh'

'jñ' is pronounced as 'ny'

The letters d-h and t-h written together are pronounced separately, as in 'madhouse' and 'pothouse'.

The 'g' in Gita is hard as in 'get'.

Vowels are as follows:

a—short as in English 'but' or long as in 'father'

e—long as in 'they'

i—short as in 'pin' or long as in 'pique'

o—long as in 'home'

u—short as in 'pull' or long as in 'rule'

The final 'a' is often omitted from proper names (Arjun for Arjuna) if the rhythm would bring a stress to this letter which is unstressed and may be unpronounced; Arjuna is stressed on the first syllable. Efforts have been made to ensure that the English stress falls on the correct syllable in Sanskrit names, but this is not always possible in rhythmic verse, especially in the list of names in chapter 1. For false stress on some names indulgence is asked of the reader; this stress does not affect the meaning of the lines.